Progressive Steps

A Novel Approach to Effective Software Upgrades

Craig Poulson
&
Alison Brown

ISBN: 1-4664-9395-X
ISBN-13: 9781466493957

Contents

1

Chuck could hear Henrich Sorenson's voice from the conference room before he turned the corner. He winced; Chuck hated being late for meetings. Taking a deep breath, he pushed through the door and sat down in the first available seat.

"So nice of you to join us," Tony Chandler said from the head of the table. Chuck mumbled his apologies as he set up his laptop. The battery light was blinking; he'd forgotten to charge it again. How could everything go wrong on the same day? Chuck looked behind him for an outlet; of course, there were none on that wall. He just had to hope the battery would outlast the meeting.

"Basically," Henrich continued, encouraged by a nod from Tony, "we know our new graphical user interface is only designed to handle a couple of the high-priority-use cases, and I feel confident that we will get slammed by the testers if we go into testing now."

"So true," Jess Alberguard said, opening his eyes halfway. As usual, he was leaning his head on his hand, looking most of the way asleep. "The process definition team keeps giving us new requirements from other use cases. Even if we had figured out how to clean up and migrate their data, we don't have the capacity to do all of the things they want, especially when they keep changing their minds about what exactly it is that they want."

Everyone nodded.

"The deployment plans aren't anywhere near done either," Raj Pulitaskar said, looking up from his doodles. "If you remember, Tony, I mentioned to you last week that the engineering supervisors haven't committed to the implementation dates. If we walked into their offices and tried to deploy it now, they would fight us on every step, not to mention the months we'd spend troubleshooting."

"No." Tony was shaking his head when everyone turned to stare at him. "We need it ready for implementation in three weeks."

There was a confused cacophony of voices.

"Three weeks!"

"But that's impossible—"

"The testing alone—"

"There's no way—"

Chuck just stared at his screen. Three weeks. Three weeks to get a mess of underdeveloped software into implementation. He closed his eyes. His family would hate this. Chuck had been pulling enough long hours lately that he barely saw Felice and Little Bob, and Julie and Ben weren't too happy with his last-minute appearances either. And Cathy would be furious.

Still, Thanksgiving was coming up. Two whole days off and a weekend to boot. He'd spend some time with them then and make it up to them. They could do some fun things—go to the zoo, go out to eat. That would help.

"Three weeks." Tony's voice cut through the chatter. "Actually, a little less. We'll be doing the implementation Thanksgiving weekend."

"Thanksgiving?" Chuck couldn't keep from sounding utterly shocked. Tony turned to him.

"It's the only time no one's using the system for long enough to allow us to install everything." His mouth twisted. "That way, the engineering supervisors won't have to give up any production time. We'll make the decision for them. They won't be able to argue because, so far, they have only fought us on losing production time. And the director needs it done before the end-of-the-year review. Ergo, Thanksgiving."

There was a moment of silence. Chuck felt like he'd been socked in the stomach. What was he going to do now?

"Right." Tony snapped his laptop closed and rose. "That's it. We will be ready for implementation Thanksgiving weekend." He strode from the room without a backward glance.

Mechanically, Chuck started putting his laptop in its case. Around him, the buzz of voices picked up again, but he tried not to listen. He took a deep breath and let it out slowly. Then he stood up and headed for his desk. There was plenty of work to do.

***

Chuck's fingers drummed idly over the keys as he stared off into space. He caught himself and looked at the clock; still half an hour until he was supposed to go home. Chuck tried to force himself to get back to work, but it was a losing battle.

His eyes kept wandering to the picture of his family on the corner of his desk. He looked at it: Ben with his hair a mess and a missing front tooth; Julie smiling demurely (she had just learned the word and was trying to act it, at least until Ben did something and she blew up); Felice not looking at the camera, as usual; and Little Bob smiling in Cathy's arms. The Strauss Family was printed in fancy lettering across the bottom. Chuck smiled at the photograph. It was old, of course—how long ago had Ben's tooth grown back in, anyway?—and he needed to replace it, but it was his favorite.

He sighed and looked back at the computer screen. He'd been planning to spend some time with them this Thanksgiving to make up for how busy he'd been lately. Now they wouldn't even get that.

A chair squealed loudly as someone pushed it back. Chuck winced as Henrich swore.

"Why can't we get some decent chairs in this place?" he demanded, half to himself, as he walked behind Chuck.

Chuck craned his neck to look up and back. "Maybe the new office will have better ones."

"If we ever get there," Jon Richet grumbled from his desk beside Chuck's. "It wasn't mentioned at the meeting, after all."

"Some meeting," Henrich said sarcastically. He sounded as annoyed as Jon, and Chuck couldn't blame him. "Working Thanksgiving!"

"I haven't worked here long," Susie Folsom chimed in, "but it seems like we work over just about every holiday." She glanced around. "Or is that my imagination?"

"Not every holiday," Chuck started to say, and then he stopped to reflect. "Just...every holiday when we actually get the system ready for an upgrade on time." He smiled wryly. "So, I guess that would be every holiday if the director had his way. Sometimes I'm just as glad that we don't get everything done on time."

"Yeah, I guess you would be. That seems rough, though. They ought to just put it in the job description, as part of the hiring agreement, if they're going to do it that way."

Jess's voice suddenly echoed over to them. "Can't do that, mate; they'd have to pay us more money. They're already trying to cut our salaries wherever they can; they certainly don't want us to have an excuse to ask for more."

"I thought that it was just your salary they cut," Chuck joked. "Because you're Australian."

Henrich smiled and left while Chuck and Jess bantered.

"Too right," Jess said. "There's no equality in these parts for a poor lad from Down Under. But just wait: you'll be next. 'He who does not take a stand against oppression is next to be oppressed.'"

Chuck paused. "Is that a real quote or did you make it up?"

"Now, why couldn't something I made up be a real quote?" Jess demanded in injured tones. "I'm quotable, I'll have you know. Except maybe to you prejudiced Americans. Racism! I'm out of here!"

Chuck was the first to break up with laughter. Jess grinned at him as he made his way to the coffeepot.

Shaking his head, Chuck turned back to Susie. "Well, if you want to believe Jess's conspiracy theory, go right ahead. But the company really does need this upgrade. The competition is get pretty stiff. They have to become more efficient to survive, and one of their biggest wastes of time is searching for data. Remember, our studies estimate twenty-three percent of engineering time can be shaved off if the system provides the data they need when they need it. And if we have to do it over Thanksgiving to get it done, that's just the way it is."

"But it isn't," interjected a new voice. Surprised, Chuck turned to see Raj coming up behind him.

"What do you mean?" Susie asked, looking from Chuck to Raj.

"We don't have to work through Thanksgiving just to help out the company," Raj said, gesturing to Chuck's computer screen. "All of that is just a lot of busy work. By the time we actually get the upgrade in place, it won't make any real difference."

"What?" Chuck stared at him. "Of course it will! This upgrade is going to save the users tons of time—how can it not make a difference?"

"Sure, we're providing a potential for improvements," Raj said, "but it's taken so long for us to create this special search engine GUI that it's built upon obsolete software and out-of-date processes. We'll never keep up with the base software revisions or with the corresponding new ways of doing things. It just takes us too long to change. Besides, frankly, we're only making educated guesses about how users will use it. We just don't have frequent enough touch points with the users. So, even though it is a great idea, we don't have a process in place to fine-tune it until it works."

"Well, all the more reason to do it at Thanksgiving, then," Chuck said. "We need to get it in place as soon as possible to get all the benefit we can out of it."

Raj shook his head. "The only reason we have to get this in place by Thanksgiving is because the director's bonus is riding on that deadline," he said flatly. "Of course, it'll do some good whenever we upgrade, but working over Thanksgiving for 'the good of the company'? Hah. It's for the good of the director's wallet."

Chuck couldn't formulate a response. He'd never heard Raj speak so bitterly about anyone. Jon, of course, was nodding agreement. "Exactly," he said. "That's just what I've been saying."

Raj didn't even look surprised to find he was agreeing with Jon. "I've thought about it, and I honestly can't come up with any other reason to get this done over Thanksgiving weekend. And I know that the director loses his bonus if we don't pull through on the date. Tony told me that one himself."

Chuck glanced toward Tony's door, aghast. Why would he do something like that? Of course, following through on the director's plans was what they did, but making them work over Thanksgiving for no better reason? That seemed unusually low.

When he turned back, Raj had already turned to leave. Chuck swallowed, wanting to call him back, to ask him more, but what could he say?

Jon was smirking. "What have I always said? They're just trying to line their pockets."

Chuck closed his computer and shoved it into his bag. He didn't want to have to deal with this. Without even looking at the clock, he left.

2

Chuck mustered a smile as he walked through the garage door. "I'm home!" he called to the quiet house.

"Dad!" Feet pounded down the stairs, and Felice flew around the corner and into his arms.

Chuck's smile became real as he lifted the girl and mock groaned.

"When did you get to be so big?" he demanded. "I can't even lift you!" He sagged to the floor.

"Dad's home!" Ben crashed into them, not even bothering to try to stop. "Dad, will you help me with my Pinewood Derby car tonight? All the other boys are almost finished with theirs."

"Sure, Ben," Chuck said. "We'll get some work done tonight, get caught up. Did you make up those plans like I asked you to?" Ben nodded, but before he could reply, Julie rounded the corner, carrying the baby. "Want to go see Daddy, Little Bob?" she asked. "Daddy's home now, so don't cry. Daddy's here."

Chuck fought his way free of the two children and picked up Little Bob. "Hiya, big guy," he said, raising the baby above his head. "Have you been a good boy today?"

"Not particularly." Cathy's voice was weary, and Chuck transferred Little Bob to his hip and moved to kiss her.

"Rough day?" he asked sympathetically.

She glared at the kids. "Should I tell your dad what you've been up to today?"

Julie, Ben, and Felice started talking at once.

"It wasn't my fault!"

"I was trying to do my homework, and he—"

"Don't listen to a word he says, Dad; he's not telling the truth."

"What are you talking about? It was all your fault!"

Little Bob decided that this was fun and started yelling nonsense at the top of his lungs.

8

"All right, all right," Chuck laughed. "It doesn't matter now whose fault it was. Let's help Mom get dinner on the table. Is it set?"

The kids looked at each other with guilty faces.

"It's Julie's turn," Ben said.

"It is not! It's your turn, you little brat. You traded with me last week, remember? So you could work on that stupid Pinewood Derby car?"

"It's not stupid! And I didn't trade you; you wouldn't trade, so I did it myself. So it is so your turn."

"Kids!" Chuck intervened, seeing that the exchange was wearing on Cathy's already frayed nerves. "Let's all go in there and help, all right? It won't take long if we all do something."

There were glares and murmurs, but no one said anything aloud as they headed into the kitchen. Cathy rolled her eyes.

"It was a half-day, and they've been getting on each other's nerves all afternoon," she explained. "And mine. I can't wait to send them back tomorrow."

He chuckled. "Thank goodness for school." They'd made their way into the kitchen, and he reached up to grab two glasses. "What is that wonderful smell?"

Cathy opened the oven and pulled out a dish of enchiladas.

"Mexican tonight," she said. "It was easiest."

"Sounds fabulous to me." He put the cups on the table and went back for more, trying to keep Little Bob from grabbing anything.

The kids didn't do much toward setting the table—he brought plates and napkins, after the cups—but they were all gathered around in a surprisingly short amount of time. Chuck leaned over his plate and inhaled deeply, eyes closed.

"What a heavenly aroma," he said.

The kids giggled. Felice tried to lean down and smell her plate, and dipped her nose in the sauce. Frowning, she swiped at her nose with the back of her hand, and, before her parents could intervene, wiped her hand on her pants. Cathy sighed. "People will never believe that I tried to teach them manners."

"They'll grow into them," Chuck said as he took a big bite of enchilada. "Mmm, it tastes even better than it smells."

"How was your day, honey?" Cathy asked as she cut Little Bob's enchilada into bite-sized pieces.

Chuck took a deep breath, all appreciation for the enchiladas gone.

"I'm afraid I got some bad news," he said.

Cathy stopped cutting and turned to look at him.

He looked down at his plate. "I'm...well, we're doing a software upgrade, and I guess the only time we can do it is, over Thanksgiving weekend." He looked around. Everyone was staring at him. "So, I'll be working over Thanksgiving. Sorry, guys."

"How come?" Ben demanded. "It's not fair. They can't make you work over Thanksgiving. It's a public holiday."

"Not fair," Felice agreed. "I want Thanksgiving!"

"You'll have Thanksgiving, Felice; Daddy just won't be there," Chuck tried to explain, but the kids didn't look any happier.

"You know what you should do, Dad?" Julie suggested. "You should go on strike—like they used to in the olden days when people made them work too long and didn't pay them enough. You march around with signs and say you're not coming back to work until they give you Thanksgiving. There's a picture in my history book. I'll show you. You just do like them."

Chuck tried to smile at her. "Thanks, Jules, but it doesn't work like that anymore. I can't go on strike. I have to work."

"But it's not fair," Julie insisted. "You have to tell them so!"

"Yeah," Ben agreed. "Isn't it, like, illegal to work on Thanksgiving? That's what a holiday means, after all."

"Don't work," Felice said. "I want Thanksgiving! I want Thanksgiving with Daddy!"

Chuck glanced at Cathy, hoping for some support, but she just sat there expressionless, dispassionately eating her enchilada. His heart dropped. He'd assumed that she, at least, would understand why he had to work. But Chuck could tell she was very disappointed, even angry.

"Come on, Dad," Ben urged. "Don't go! Have Mom call you in sick."

Chuck would have laughed at that one, if he hadn't been feeling an almost overwhelming urge to cry. His kids looked so upset.

"We'll do something special for Christmas," he offered, but they refused to listen. For the rest of the meal, they came up with more and more absurd strategies to get out of working that day, and he was grateful when it was over.

"I need to change my clothes," he announced and escaped up to the bedroom.

3

Chuck looked around the new office and smiled. They'd finally managed to get all their stuff moved over. What a job that had been! Murphy's Law had struck. They'd been waiting to get into the new office for about a year. Of course, they were forced to move when they should have been preparing for the implementation. It had taken them all day, but now, it was done.

The new office was a lot nicer than the old one. He sat down at his desk, noting with satisfaction that the chair didn't make a sound—no chance that this one would break and drop him to the ground. There was even room for people to maneuver around without always bumping into each other's chairs.

"Looks good, everyone," Tony said, surveying the room. "It took a while, but finally I got the directors to give in. We're living in luxury now!"

Everyone laughed, and Jess raised his coffee mug in a toast. "To our new office!"

Water bottles, coffee mugs, and other assorted drinking utensils were raised to meet his. "Our office!" A splash of water from one over-filled cup splashed to the ground. Raj grimaced.

"Glad it missed my desk!"

It had been close, but there were no complaints. "Now it's duly toasted and baptized," Jess said. "Let's get out of here!"

More laughter accompanied their departure.

***

The next morning, Tony interrupted Chuck in the middle of his work. "Come on, let's go."

"Go where?" Chuck swiveled his chair around, surprised, to meet Tony's eyes.

"To meet with the consultants the power-train group hired, of course. I told you, they want to ask you about the common work processes."

Chuck frowned, thoughts darting frantically through his mind. He couldn't remember Tony mentioning any such thing. How had he forgotten?

"I did tell you, didn't I?" Tony sounded a little uncertain.

"I don't think so. I don't remember it."

Tony shrugged it off. "Well, come on. They're waiting for us."

Chuck stuffed his computer in his bag and hurried after Tony, wondering how much good this was really going to do. He remembered his own first assignment documenting business processes at a plant in Malaysia. He'd been the one doing the interviewing, but the experience was a nightmare. Once he'd documented an explanation from one expert, another would come in and refute the previous explanation by saying it applied only in one specialized case, and that things were totally different in another part of the company. These consultants were hired to sit in a room until they had gathered everyone's feedback on how the processes were working and then recommend how improvements could be made. How could this be useful?

He pushed his thoughts aside as he entered the conference room. The three men and two women looked up from their computers and greeted them. As Chuck connected his laptop to the projector and opened the PowerPoint presentation, hoping that this would be over with quickly.

"Our team is designing a new Graphical User Interface, or GUI, that will allow engineers to find data on any part through a simple search," he began. Chuck didn't like to give presentations without rehearsing, but this basic introduction he'd given so often, he thought he could do it in his sleep.

The consultants listened politely, but he got the impression that they'd heard this information before. He moved through the slides as quickly as possible. When he reached the end, he smiled at them. "So, those are the basics. What specific questions do you have?"

"Metrics—how many times, how many people, how long on average, how long maximum, etc."

The questions went on and on, wanting details on how possible use cases might affect the process. He guessed as best he could, knowing how it would affect the project to show any uncertainty. They took copious notes, and he could see their reports growing longer by the minute. He wanted to shake his head. How long would it take them to document the "as-is" and then develop the "to-be" process? Documentation would be nearing completion when the new software release got implemented and changed all of the processes. But, of course, they were being paid to redesign based on the current processes, so he gave them his best guesses. He thought about what Jess might have said to them.

His head was aching by the time they were through. He took two ibuprofen as he sat down and reopened the content documents for the upcoming new release. The complex custom code of the work around they'd developed stared back at him.

"Ridiculous, isn't it?" Jess said over his shoulder.

Chuck glanced up at him. "What?"

"That we won't be running our spatial searches on the upcoming release of the base code. We wouldn't need half of our customizations if we could."

"I know," Chuck sighed. "I was so excited when I realized that the new version had the capability to do almost everything we needed!"

"Weren't we all, mate?" Jess chuckled. "Well, it keeps us on our toes! We'll never be out of a job so long as the company implements so slowly." He continued on his way out of the room.

Chuck looked around and saw that most of the group had left. He glanced at his watch; it was lunchtime. With his stomach in knots from the stress, he dug his lunch out. He didn't really feel hungry, but he needed to eat something. But he kept looking over the documents as he ate.

Sometime after lunch, an alarm sounded on his phone. It was time for another conference call, this one on application licensing. He dialed in and announced himself, then sat back to listen.

"All right, Nathan," the call director said, already sounding frustrated. "Have we made any progress on buying the licenses we need? It's been a year, and users are starting to get impatient."

"I found this great bundle last week," Nathan said excitedly. "It has almost all of the functions we need, for a very good price."

"And how many functions we don't need?" a voice interjected in a snide tone.

"You know there are always a few," Nathan said, with forced patience. "But everyone knows you get the best long-term deal with bundles."

"What exactly is in this one?" the call host cut in.

Nathan listed quite a few of the applications they needed. Chuck's eyebrows raised as the list continued, and he nodded. It sounded like a good deal.

Nathan then moved to the unnecessary applications also included in the bundle. Chuck tensed; one of the vital functions to his team's design hadn't yet been mentioned. He turned off the mute on his phone and spoke up as soon as Nathan finished.

"Have you found the change management module?" Chuck asked.

Nathan's voice was edged with tension. "Not yet. You can't expect everything in one bundle. But I'm looking into others that have it."

Chuck decided to stop pushing him; the man was already under enough stress. But the exchange left Chuck uneasy. He remembered his involvement in a project to develop a process using an open license key, and no one realized that one of the applications used in the process had never actually been purchased. It wasn't until they'd tried the process on a computer with a standard license that it failed. It had taken six months to buy the license they needed to actually use their process. He didn't want anything like that happening with the new search methods.

But Nathan had been reminded. Chuck put the phone back on mute and opened the content documents again, only listening with half his attention. He fell back to his habit of listing and then attempting to prioritize the tasks he had waiting for him—hoping against hope that he would find a clever way to make it look doable. *Hmmm,* Chuck thought, *this is such a big release, coordinating the user-acceptance testing will be a nightmare.* He already had a plan that was moving forward, but if it was going to succeed, he needed to put a lot of effort into communication and coordination. One of his major problems was that of avoiding just taking whomever the managers could send—they were always the ones you did not want to do testing. And then along the user-acceptance testing lines, Chuck needed to refine the steps in the use cases. He'd learned a lot from his initial user evaluation, and they weren't going to use the searches like the software architects intended. They had some different nuances. He couldn't even begin to take the time now to explore how the more inventive, but probably more productive, users would employ the system. Even so, the decisions he made now would make it difficult to change later. But the biggest elephant in the room was drafting a plan on how to coordinate the implementation within the timeframe and other constraints that the IT organization imposed upon them. That reminded him of the work Tony and Raj were attempting, which was to get the supervisors on board with new ways of doing things.

4

"So this is where you've been hiding." Chuck looked up from his research into possible Christmas destinations to see Cathy standing in the door, Little Bob on her hip. He looked back down at the screen and realized that he'd spent over an hour on the Internet.

"Sorry, honey. I got distracted," he said, closing the screen and setting the laptop aside. He stood up and went to take the baby from her. "How ya doing, big guy?" He wrinkled his nose at the smell emanating from the baby's diaper.

"He's the only one not upset with the fact that you won't be here for Thanksgiving." Cathy stalked over to the changing table and pulled out a fresh diaper and wet wipes.

He followed her over, wondering what to say to convince her. "Honey, I'm sorry. You know I am." He laid the baby down and stripped the dirty diaper off him. "It's not like I volunteered to work over Thanksgiving." He knew he sounded defensive, but he couldn't stop himself from adding, "I don't have a choice."

"Yes, you do, Chuck," Cathy said, turning to look straight at him. "You always have a choice."

"But it's my job."

"It's always your job! You never have time for me or the kids because of your job. Even when you're home, you're working. And you always say that you have no choice. Well, I'm sick of it. Make a choice! Do something about this job."

Chuck couldn't think of what to say. He fastened the new diaper as he struggled to collect his thoughts. "What do you mean?"

"It's your job! Make changes to it so it suits you," Cathy shot back. "I refuse to believe that everyone else on your team is working as many hours as you are. In fact, I know they're not, because you've said so. You're the only one who seems to find that your job takes twelve hours a day. Cut back! The company can handle it. Do what they hired you for, not twice as much."

Chuck shook his head. "Cathy, it's not like that. I'm not just doing extra work. It's necessary."

"Oh?" The look in her eye made him back off.

"Of course, it's important to be home with you and the kids, too. I know that." He took a breath. "I'll try harder to be home more evenings, spend more time with you and the kids. Would that help?"

"You always say that, Chuck, but it only lasts a few days." She sighed. "But yes, it would help—if you did it."

"I will," he insisted, stung by her accusations. "I mean, things are going to be pretty crazy through Thanksgiving, but-"

She threw her hands up and turned away. "But after that? Then things will get busy until Christmas, but you'll be here for the vacation, maybe, and next year—oh, wait, next year all the new goals and quotas for the year will be up and, oh no, they'll be driving you harder than ever. But someday, surely, you'll get a break! And then you'll spend a little time at home. When? When Little Bob's in college?"

He glared at her back. "That's not fair, Cathy, and you know it."

"What you're doing to us isn't fair, Chuck! We need you here now, not in a while when things slow down at work. They never will! Haven't you noticed that? You have to make time for what's important to you."

He realized that his teeth were clenched and forced himself to relax, taking a slow breath. "Look, that's not the point right now. I said I'd try to spend more time with you and the kids, all right? But that won't change Thanksgiving."

Cathy turned back around to face him. "Can't you find some way out of that?"

"What? Have you call me in sick, like Ben said?" He laughed bitterly. "That won't work, Cathy. I have to go in. It's a big upgrade, they're going to need me."

"Then quit." She said it almost casually, but he could see the look in her eyes after she said it, knew she was worried at the thought.

"I can't, honey." He tried to smile. "You want me home but not like that. We need this job."

She sighed. "I know. But isn't there some way to keep this job without working over Thanksgiving?"

He walked over and put an arm around her. "It's just one day, honey. It'll be OK."

"It's more than that to me, Chuck."

He knew that. Thanksgiving was Cathy's favorite holiday, and to her, it epitomized family togetherness.

"I'm sorry, honey, but there's nothing I can do about it."

"Why not?" This time she didn't sound angry, but thoughtful. "There must be some way out of it, Chuck. Get your stuff done early so that you don't have to work that day."

He laughed. "I thought you didn't want me working all the time. Even working twenty-four hours a day, I don't think I could do that."

"Well, talk to Tony. Tell him you have to be home for Thanksgiving. Couldn't you do the upgrade at night? I'd let you sleep the day after, if I had you for Thanksgiving."

He smiled but shook his head. "It doesn't work like that, hon."

"Chuck, you're giving up too easily. You can make this work. I know you can." She leaned over to kiss him lightly. "I married you because I knew you were a smart man. Now use those brains to figure out some way to not work on Thanksgiving."

He sighed. "I wish I could. I really do."

She was silent for a moment. When she spoke again, it was obvious that she'd decided to change tactics. "Will you explain to me exactly why you have to work on Thanksgiving? What is it that you'll be doing?"

"All right," he said, surprised. It took a minute to compose his thoughts. "You know how the customer uses my company's software to manage their data?"

She nodded.

"Well, my team figures out how to setup the software to make their common processes more efficient, making it more responsive to the needs of the users. We've come up with some ways to make it better, so we're going to put this better way of using the software into place."

"I get that," Cathy said. "What I don't understand is why that means that you need to work on Thanksgiving Day. No one's using your software then."

"Exactly. Our setup is based on a newer version of the base software so we need to delete the old version from all the computers and put in a new one set up correctly. You remember when Ben installed that game on the computer and it froze up for an hour? It'll be like that, only much longer. So we have to do it when no one's online."

"Well, why don't you just set it to install and then leave, like you do with a game?"

He smiled. "I wish we could. Unfortunately, it needs constant supervision. It isn't all bundled into a simple installation package. We have to perform a whole bunch of steps, so many that it will take a couple of days."

She frowned. "So why does it have to take all weekend?"

"Because there are so many changes we're making. We've been working on these improvements for over a year, and there are a lot of things that we need to change now."

She gnawed the inside of her lip. He knew that gesture well; she always did it when she was thinking over something she didn't like. He wasn't sure whether she even knew she was doing it. "So why didn't you install those improvements little by little, as you went along?"

He opened his mouth to answer, and then paused. All he could think to say was, *That's the way it's done.* Suddenly, he found himself wondering if that was a good enough reason. Could there be another way?

"Well," he said slowly, thinking it over, "because then we'd have to take the system offline every few weeks. It would be ridiculous."

She started to say something, but he was on a roll now and kept going. "And besides, we don't have any way to make those changes on a regular basis. There are a lot of checks and balances required before implementation. They used to make changes whenever they had new software, and it caused chaos."

"All right," she finally said. "I was just thinking—it feels like you guys are playing this game in fits and starts. You work really hard for a weekend, do nothing for a while, then develop a whole backlog of improvements waiting to be made, and then you finally work over a holiday to put in all the improvements you've needed for years. It seems really stupid because you don't even have any idea if the users like what you're doing. Then when you finally give it to them in a big bang, how do you know if they even use it?"

"That's life," he said. "It's like fixing up the house. We let the showerhead get leakier and leakier until, finally, we can't take it anymore, and we hire someone to tear up the bathroom and replace the shower and mess up our lives for three days. And then we're satisfied for a while."

"No, it's like building a new house every year. It just seems like computers should make it easier, rather than harder, to do that kind of thing. You should get fixes and benefits faster than you do from a plumbing contractor who physically has to rip out tile."

He laughed. "Shows how much you know about computers. They usually make things harder, not easier."

But, suddenly, she was annoyed with him. "Yes, I've noticed. They're tearing our family apart."

He tried to backpedal. "Honey, I was just-"

"Look, Chuck. You're not even making an effort to get out of working on Thanksgiving. I know my ideas aren't the best—I don't have the education you do in this field—but at least I'm trying. I don't even have any resources, and I'm trying, while you don't even make the least bit of effort! You just accept it—that's the way life is—and you don't even try. You can do something about this, Chuck! And I don't want you to just give in without a fight."

"What do you think I've been doing?" he said, hurt by her tone. "I've been thinking about this all afternoon! I talked to the guys about it at work. They don't want to work Thanksgiving, either, but they know as well as I do that there's no way out of it. We're stuck. I've tried to come up with ideas, but not one of them has the least chance of working."

"Then you're not trying hard enough."

"Cathy, that's not fair." He stood up, not wanting to fight. "I'll go read the kids their bedtime story."

"Fine, ignore it," she snapped. "End our conversation. I'll be quiet. But that doesn't mean I like it. And I still want you to come up with some way to get out of working over Thanksgiving."

He walked out the door, gritting his teeth to prevent the anger from spilling out.

5

The next morning, Chuck was the first one to arrive. He was still thinking about Cathy's insistence that he get out of working over Thanksgiving, and her idea of upgrading a little at a time. Preoccupied, he walked toward the old office and almost in the door before he realized what he was doing. Shaking his head at his own absent-mindedness, he turned and headed the other way.

He saw Raj standing in the door before he got there. "Good morning," he started to call, but stopped as he realized that something was wrong. Why was Raj just standing there like that?

Raj turned to face him. "Not so good," he answered sourly, stepping aside and gesturing into the room.

Chuck looked inside and bit back a curse. The room was a disaster area. The carpet was soaked through; there were even puddles in places that he wouldn't want to walk through without boots. His chair was visible from the door; the seat cradled a lake of its own. And his desk-

Luckily, he hadn't left anything valuable out on his desk. It was only a few things, but not even they escaped unscathed. The worst was the picture of his family. Even from the door, he could see the streaking on the photo. The cheap frame wasn't enough to keep out the water.

"What happened?" he said in shock.

"Looks like our lovely office has some flaws," was all Raj said.

They went inside and started straightening things up. Raj went to the bathroom for a double handful of paper towels and they started mopping up the desks. By common consent, they ignored the central table and the floor for a while.

Expressions of shock and outrage from the doorway alerted them to the fact that their co-workers had arrived. Jon and Henrich looked furious. Susie wasn't far behind them; she looked like she was about to cry. Even Jess woke up when he stepped inside the room without looking and hit a puddle that splashed up to his ankle.

"What the-" Jess stopped as he looked around the room. When he spoke again, it was quiet. "What happened?"

"What do you think?" Jon was not trying to hide his bitterness. He had a drawer open in his desk and was fishing out documents that had been only partially protected. He draped them over his desk, and then started working his way up the wall. The sodden papers clung to whatever they touched; Chuck wondered if they would leave ink stains on the nice, new walls. At the moment, he hoped they did.

Jess made his way carefully around the table to his desk, dodging standing water. Chuck hadn't dared venture over that way yet; Jess had picked a desk directly under a window, and Chuck was afraid of what he'd see.

An angry cry confirmed Chuck's fears, as Jess let fly with inventive stream of profanity. "My work!" he moaned, his voice withering from furious to heartbroken.

Chuck sloshed over to take a look. His feet were already wet, so there was no need to avoid the puddles. He could see why his co-worker was so upset. Jess followed the piling method of filing: stacks of paper that he insisted were carefully organized covered his desk, some rising to precarious heights. Now they were all flatter, compressed by the water weight.

"Is this for real?" Jess demanded weakly. "Please tell me I'm dreaming."

Chuck prodded a pile of paper gingerly. "I'm afraid not," he said. "I'm not sure whether or not this is salvageable, Jess."

Jess gritted his teeth, then turned and kicked the leg of the desk. The piles shifted, and Chuck reached out hurriedly to keep them in place.

"Don't bother," Jess said. "They're ruined anyway."

Embarrassed, Chuck looked away. "Maybe if I open a window, we'll get some stuff dried up in here," he suggested to the room at large.

The windows, of course, were next to impossible to open. Why the windows leaked but wouldn't open was beyond Chuck; undoubtedly, some marvel of modern engineering. He ended up hammering at the lock with the heel of his hand until it gave. Then, of course, there was nowhere to get a grip on it to raise the sash. *Who cares?* he thought grimly, placed his palms flat on the pane, fingers jammed against the small ridge at the top, and pushed upward. It didn't budge. He reset his feet, crouched lower, and pushed again, this time with a grunt. The window shifted upward. Wedging his fingers into the crack at the bottom, he heaved again. Suddenly, it shot upward, startling him so much that he almost let it fall down again. Hurriedly, he flipped the latch back into place.

A breeze pushed passed him, and he smiled in relief. That would help.

"Hey!" Jon shouted from the other side of the room. "My papers!"

Chuck turned around to see the wind lift the papers he had laid out to dry off the desk and wall and deposit them gently, and with unerring accuracy, into a puddle.

Jon glared around the room. "What idiot opened that window?"

Chuck bit his lip, not wanting to speak up. It was Jess who answered. "We're trying to get it dry in here. What were you thinking, putting those things where they could blow away?"

"Look, Jess, you may think you know more than the rest of us, but let me assure you that I am not..."

"What's going on here?"

Chuck had never been so glad to hear Tony's voice. Jon and Jess were both explaining at once, trying to outdo each other in describing their annoyance with the engineers who had built the new office. Susie's desk was mostly dry, Chuck saw; she was seated, pretending to be engrossed in her computer, but he could see her glancing around to listen. Raj and Henrich were both keeping quiet.

"And then he opened the stupid window and sent my documents-"

"I didn't open that window, but I think it was a-"

"Those were the tester's review comments; it'll take days to call the testers to ask if they remember what they wrote-"

"Yeah, well, my entire desk is soaked through; you want to talk about how long it'll take to redo that work?"

"All right!" Tony cut them both off. Everyone turned to look at him. "So we've got some problems here. We can handle it. Let's get all of the wet paper out of here and try to find somewhere dry to set it. Then we can let the wind dry out the chairs and carpets."

"Do you think this will keep happening, Tony?" Chuck asked as everyone turned to get back to work. "Last year, it rained for half of November. We can't do this every day."

"I might as well just dump this all in the trash right now," Jess grumbled. "I'm not putting up with this!"

"I'm sure we'll get it under control," Tony said confidently. "Come on, let's try and put things where they'll stay dry."

The team noticed that there were areas of the room that had mostly escaped the flooding. They moved desks and chairs around the conference tables, trying to keep them out of the worst of the water. Jess's was the hardest, immersed as it was in the largest puddle and weighed down with sodden paper. It took all of them working together to carry it.

When they were done, they surveyed the new arrangement. Jess started to laugh wryly. "We look like a bunch of sheep huddling together out of the wind," he said, gesturing the desks squeezed into one corner of the room. The worst areas under the windows were cordoned off by equally wet chairs. Tony made a run to get them some replacement chairs; none of them asked where from.

Chuck grinned, fatigued before the workday even started. "Well, two hours later, we can finally start work," he said. "Good morning, everyone."

Jess muttered something about what kind of a morning it was and headed out of the room, probably for more coffee. Chuck and Susie sat down next to each other. Susie was immediately buried in her work. Chuck opened his documents, but he couldn't concentrate. Cathy's ideas kept coming to mind. He still hadn't worked out how they could be feasible, and he was reaching the end of his own inventiveness. He needed some outside help.

When Jess came back in, he caught him before he could make his way to his desk. "Can I talk to you for a sec?" he asked.

Jess took a long drink of his coffee. "Sure, what's up?"

Chuck took a deep breath, wondering where to start. Behind him, Susie moved off to talk to Henrich and Jon; Chuck was relieved not to have to pitch his plan to both of them at once.

"I was thinking about working over Thanksgiving," he said.

Jess rolled his eyes. "Don't remind me," he grumbled. "That's ridiculous."

"Yeah, well, that's what my family thinks, too," Chuck said. "So I've been thinking about it. Why do we have to do these huge upgrades anyway? Why not just roll in small improvements all the time?"

To his surprise, Jess burst out laughing. "That'd be the day," he said, patting Chuck on the shoulder. "We don't want to go back to that."

"Back to what?"

"Anarchy," Jess said, gesturing expansively. "Disaster. Complete and unmitigated chaos."

"I wasn't here back then. What was it like, Jess?"

Finally, Jess settled into a detailed explanation. "They used to let people install changes to the software on their personal computers anytime they wanted, oh, about ten years ago. Anyone who came up with a good idea could put it in."

Chuck frowned. "Having administrative privileges sounds like a good idea to me," he said with a sarcastic smile; from Jess's reaction, it obviously was not.

"That's what they thought at first," Jess said. "Then they started getting changes made all the time, changes no one knew about or could track. People could show up at work and find the application they'd been using inoperable, and they couldn't figure out how to get it working again. Oh, and you know how engineers like to write code in their spare time? Yep, they did, but they didn't have time to generalize it. Some major projects stalled because of bugs in their unsupported code. No one could get anything done. Utter chaos, as I said."

"Oh." Chuck digested Jess's logistical horror story. "I guess that would be pretty bad."

"That's why we have a formal change process," Jess said, "It's a pain, but at least everyone knows what's going on. Buy software from a vendor, follow the process for any changes…it all works."

"On the other hand, software vendors don't really sell what we actually need," Chuck said. "We used to have our own software development divisions writing code to meet our requirements. We switched to vendors to save money but unfortunately now we think once we buy it, it's 'done'. No one is changing fast enough to keep up with industry needs."

Jess stood up. "True enough, mate. Good luck changing the world!"

Chuck shook his head as Jess sauntered off. He was right; imagining a utopia did them no good. With a sigh he turned back to his real work.

6

Chuck closed his menu and passed it to the server. As she left, Cathy smiled at him. "This was a good idea. It's been a long time since we've gone out to eat."

He smiled back, glad that his plan was working, thus far at least. Cathy had been warmer toward him ever since he suggested the idea, and tonight, he could almost believe that things were normal between them.

"I just hope they're quick tonight. I'm starving," Chuck said, clutching his growling stomach, theatrically.

Cathy laughed. "You should have had a snack before we left, like I did."

"I didn't anticipate it taking quite so much time to get out the door." Felice had had a breakdown, clinging to his leg and crying. They'd had to stop and soothe her, in addition to Little Bob—who automatically joined in any crying fit—before they'd managed to sneak out while Julie distracted them with candy.

"I hope she doesn't give the babysitter too much trouble," Cathy said, looking worried.

He reached across the table and gently squeezed her hand to reassure her. "They'll be fine. They all like Laura. And besides, tonight is about us. No worrying about the kids."

"All right." This time, a bigger smile from Cathy caused him to grin, too.

Just then, their server returned with a basket of bread and a dish of butter, which they descended upon in unison.

"This is wonderful," he said around a mouthful. "I'd forgotten how much I loved this place."

"Mmm-hmm," Cathy agreed, daintily nibbling her own bread. "It's been a long time."

Conversation ranged from old dates to grandiose plans for the future as they waited for their food. When the steaks arrived, Chuck dug in immediately, but Cathy paused before starting to cut.

"You know, I was thinking," she said tentatively.

Chuck looked up at her, wondering what this portended.

"What I said the other night about doing your upgrades a little at a time, instead of all at once—are you sure it isn't possible?" She didn't sound accusatory this time but genuinely interested.

Chuck laid down his knife and fork. "Funny you should bring that up," he said. "I was thinking about it quite a bit."

"Really?" She raised her eyebrows. "What did you come up with?"

Suddenly, he felt embarrassed. "Well, I only played around with it. I don't really know. It's totally different from anything we do now, of course."

"But it is possible?" she asked eagerly.

"It might be." He raised a restraining hand. "But I don't know and I couldn't do it myself. And I just don't have enough time to explore it more." She looked upset, and he hurried to explain. "It's an interesting idea—I guess it's too interesting; that's the problem. I find myself thinking about it too much and not getting my work done. So I decided to put it on the back burner for a while."

She frowned. Deliberately picking up her silverware, she cut a bite and ate it before replying. "I think you're just giving up."

Hurt, he put his own silverware back down. "What?"

"You're just giving in to the way things have always been. You're not thinking about it." She took another bite. He couldn't think of eating; his stomach was in knots. He'd tried so hard to get this just right, he'd even thought about her ideas, and she didn't believe it? "You just don't want to have to face the chain of command at work and tell them you've had an idea."

He thought of the story he'd read to the kids the other night. "No one wants to be the one to point out that the emperor has no clothes."

"You're scared," Cathy said matter-of-factly, starting in on her baked potato.

He stared at her in shock. "What-? How?" he sputtered, unable to form a complete sentence.

"You're scared to buck authority," she said, looking up from her plate. "You have to stand up for things sometimes, Chuck."

Chuck was dumbstruck. Defiantly, he took his fork and stabbed his steak, sawing at it with the knife held in his fist. He stuck a large piece in his mouth and chewed for what seemed like an eternity. She seemed unaware of any tension and continued eating. "Oh, this is heavenly."

Silently, he forced himself to consider what Cathy had said. So he didn't want to buck the system. Who did? He wasn't a director; he didn't have the power to change the course of the company. He wasn't even a project manager. He did the grunt work. And he had to do what he was told.

"Cathy, I can't just go to the directors and tell them they're doing it wrong and that they should let me spend all my time coming up with a better way," he said. "Even if I was right, they'd have no guarantee. They won't pay for ideas when they already have a system that works."

"Well, they should," she replied. "How else are they going to stay competitive? You should at least try, Chuck. You never know; you might be surprised."

"Look, honey, it's not that I don't want to-," he started to say, but she cut him off.

"That's exactly what it is. You don't want to take the risk," Cathy said pointedly, locking her gaze on him. "What's the worst that can happen? They fire you? I've already said I'm OK with you quitting if it'll get you home for Thanksgiving."

"Cathy, be reasonable about this," he pleaded. "We don't want to risk my job. And I only said it was an interesting idea; there's no guarantee that it'll ever work."

She shook her head. "It all comes down to the same thing, Chuck. You're afraid of the risk. But this is worth it!" She was pleading now. "We need you home, Chuck. Isn't your family worth a little risk?"

He took another bite, feeling backed into a corner.

"It's delicious," she said, throwing him with the non-sequitur comment. He looked over and noticed that her plate was almost empty. He decided to take the excuse to redirect his attention to his meal and kept his mouth too full to talk for the next few minutes.

But the silence only gave him more time to think. Was she right? Honestly, he had to admit to himself that it wasn't too likely that he'd get fired for working on the idea. Being told to cut it out, that was likely, but that was all. Maybe it was worth it to keep peace in the family. He could talk to the others about it and see what they thought. If there was any way to make it feasible, Jess and Raj would know. And if not, they'd tell him, and he could tell Cathy. Same thing if Tony told him to stop; she'd have to accept it then.

"All right," he acquiesced. "I'll work on it. I'll talk to the guys and see what they think. I can't make any promises, but I will put some effort into it."

She beamed with excitement. "Wonderful!" She clasped her hands and looked off into space. "Oh, I'm so glad! I know this will work."

Chuck didn't share her confidence, but seeing the happiness on her face did make him feel good. He smiled back. "Well, I certainly hope so. It would turn things on their heads if a history major who hasn't worked outside the house in ten years came up with computer systems' implementation innovation."

She laughed. "Triumph of the liberal arts! We really can do anything we put our minds to!"

He shook his head but laughed with her. "Maybe so. You're certainly smarter than me."

"Oh, I don't know about that. I think you're pretty smart, too." Her smile turned flirtatious, and he put down his fork.

"Shall we go, brilliant lady?"

"Anywhere." She took his arm as they left the restaurant.

7

Chuck hit send on the last of the e-mails and sat back. Now, until the users replied, he didn't have to worry about their requirements. He logged into the latest GUI build to do a little quick testing. *Might as well use the time constructively*, he thought.

"Let's see how I can crash you today," he said and started toying with the search parameters. He actually was fond of this program. Engineers spent around a quarter of their time looking for data on different parts; if this GUI into the data worked properly, they could cut that down significantly. Most of the data were already related in the databases. All that they needed was a proper method to harvest the relationship indexes and a GUI to help the users quickly and easily access the data they wanted—in the format and at the level of detail they needed—without giving too much information and bogging the system down.

Unfortunately, there were still flaws. Right now, they were working on making the GUI intuitive. Someone had suggested the search should work like a wizard that walked the user through the steps. This had brought up the complaint that advanced users shouldn't be forced to go through redundant steps when they simply wanted to get back to the same data context. So, they made some changes and, of course, introduced some new bugs. He wanted to see if Henrich had resolved the last set of issues they'd encountered.

He typed in the criteria that had locked the program up last time. So far, so good. The next screen came up just fine. But when he hit "return," the page froze. He waited patiently, and then not so patiently and finally killed the application. After looking through the log files, he was pretty confident the root cause was a bug in the base code and not something with their customization.

He opened up the programming form and stared at it for a moment. He knew from experience that it would take at least a week to get a response. On the other hand, Henrich had just walked in. Chuck pushed back his chair and slogged his way across the damp carpet to Henrich's desk.

"Can you give me a hand with this?" He explained what had happened.

Henrich frowned and turned to his computer where he had the code already up. Scanning through the strings of symbols, he stopped at a point that made no sense to Chuck. Henrich grimaced. "Of course. It isn't the base code. It's my problem. I didn't anticipate you'd want to use a wild card in that field. I can straighten that out in a few minutes."

He started typing. Chuck turned away. "Thanks, Henrich."

"Wait a second," Henrich said, tapping a few more keys. "I think I've got that bug out. Try it again."

"Right." Chuck sat down and reopened the wizard. This time, the search went through without a problem. He turned and grinned at Henrich. "Perfect! Thank you."

"No problem. Just don't tell the boss."

As he turned back to his computer, Chuck shook his head at yet another ridiculous aspect of this project. Henrich was their programming expert, but they weren't supposed to actually let him program anything. He was only supposed to write up the proposals and give them to Development. Then, in about three months or whenever the guys over there got around to it, they'd get the new code. *Which was so useful then, of course,* Chuck thought sarcastically.

Or you could just give it to Henrich under the table, and he'd have it done in next to no time. "Why don't they just assign you to our team as a programmer? Put a programmer on every team and forget about Development!"

Henrich shrugged. "I've asked. But they say that for the big projects it's more cost-effective to have a central group writing the code."

"Yeah, but the turn-around time..." Chuck let the words trail off as things started falling into place. "But in the short-term, little problems are easier to solve when you put the programmers and the engineers together, right?"

Henrich looked at him like he was losing it. "Of course," he said in a tone that Julie would have used to say, "No duh, Dad."

"Thanks, Henrich!" Whirling away from the bemused programmer, Chuck ran back down the narrow aisle beside the conference table to the brainstorming whiteboard; he had to get this written down before he forgot it.

33

"Jess—" The whiteboard marker ran out of ink. He glared at it, shook it a few times but still no ink. He tossed it aside and tried the green—even worse. "Why do we never have working markers?"

"Because people leave the caps off," Susie called out from behind him.

He ignored her. The red was still working; he continued his note. "It works better to do upgrades little by little. What we really need to do is to change things as the users request them, or as soon as new features are made available in the base software. It doesn't have to be anarchy as long as WE stay in charge of the changes; we know the processes to follow to keep it in order."

Out of the corner of his eye, he saw Tony heading for the office. He quickly dropped the marker and headed for his desk. He needed to be on-task.

Susie obviously hadn't seen; she shoved her chair back to block his way. "Like that," she said. "Put the cap on that thing or we'll have no working markers left at all."

He stared at her, and she wilted slightly, moving her chair. Hurriedly, he reached back and capped the pen, then shoved his way past her and was back at his computer as Tony walked in the door.

"Good morning, everyone," Tony said as he picked his way around the chairs.

"Morning, Tony," came back the chorus. Chuck typed some random search terms into the wizard. It performed fine, of course.

Tony stopped behind him. "How's our baby doing?"

"Great," Chuck said, trying to speak lightly. "I think we've got most of the bugs out. We still have a lot of installation planning details to work out, but everyone seems to be making progress on that."

"Good, good," Tony said, moving on. "That's what we need: a bug-free installation over Thanksgiving. Then they'll be grateful we put this on their computers."

"The ingrates" seemed to be hanging off the end of his sentence. No one added it, but it was annoying that all their work was valued so little that the engineering management wouldn't even spare the time to install it.

They don't realize how much time a little change could save them, Chuck thought, and was startled by the double application, to the GUI and to his new idea. *Well, Cathy's idea*, he corrected himself, but it was starting to feel like his now. He'd started thinking a lot about it.

He realized that his hands were trembling and shook them out. He couldn't wait for Jess to come and to see what he thought.

8

It wasn't until he came back from lunch that he met with Jess. Lost in thought, he turned into the office and nearly bumped into him. Both leaned back, trying to keep the hot coffee from drenching them; the plastic lid on Jess's cup mitigating the damage.

Chuck checked to make sure he was dry and then looked eagerly up at Jess, who gestured dramatically with one of his personal markers at the whiteboard. Jess's one-word, multicolored, half-decorated response awaited: "Huh?"

Chuck had to laugh, despite feeling a little disappointed. "Sit down and I'll tell you about it," he invited, plopping into the nearest chair.

Jess took another long gulp of coffee and sat down next to him. Chuck waited for him to take another drink, and another, before his eyes finally came more than halfway open.

"What're you on about, mate?" Jess asked.

"Look," Chuck started eagerly, "I was talking to Henrich, and…" He stopped himself and shook his head. "That's starting in the wrong place. It's really simple."

Jess raised an eyebrow. "Really?"

Chuck nodded. "We don't have to…Look, what usually happens when we develop all this software, get it internally certified, and dump it on a user group?"

"They haven't the faintest idea how to use it," Jess snorted.

"Right, right, but when they do figure out how to use it?"

"They come to us whining about how it doesn't meet their needs or there're bugs in it, and we have to fix it." Jess looked annoyed at the very thought.

"Exactly. Isn't that just what we do when we get code back from Development?"

Jess laughed. "Woe unto the hypocrite, is it? All right, I suppose so. But that's why we've got Henrich."

Chuck smiled broadly and nodded. "Precisely! That's what we have to do!"

Jess just stared at him. Then he picked up his cup and drained the rest of the coffee. He set it down and looked back at Chuck. "Nope, still not getting it."

Chuck laughed, giddy with the excitement of this idea. "That's the way upgrades should work! We sketch out a broad plan and get development to regularly give us the latest base code. Then our team, including programmers, works directly with users to install it and improve it in response to their needs—instead of a giant project once or twice a year!"

"Oh." Jess just looked at him for a moment. Then he laughed and shook his head. "I'll say, mate, you don't think small, do you?"

"What?"

"I was just joking about changing the world, you know. I wasn't saying that you should actually do it."

Chuck blinked. "I guess it would be a bit difficult to implement..."

"A bit? There's an understatement if I ever heard one. You're turning the business upside down, mate."

"But it needs to be done!" Chuck exclaimed, slapping the table. "Don't you see the difference it could make?"

"Oh, sure. But it's still skirting the edge of anarchy a little too closely for my taste. Changing everything day to day—the users are going to feel like you're pulling the ground out from under them."

"No..." Chuck thought about that for a moment. "Well, maybe a little, at first. But they want us to listen to them; it's usually us hiding from them because they keep trying to change things! If we had a system that let them tell us what they needed, they'd love it."

Jess shrugged one shoulder. "Could be. But you're talking a huge change to corporate culture here. It would be crazy. Useful, definitely, but crazy."

"We could do it. Everyone agrees that open, transparent communication is important. This would actually put it into practice."

"Maybe so." Jess stood up.

"Where are you going?"

"To get more coffee. You made me use all of mine up in just five minutes' discussion." He grinned. "I can't wait to see what you come up with next."

Somehow, Chuck managed to concentrate on the detailed implementation steps, working out the critical path, while Jess was gone. In fact, he was so immersed in his own thoughts that he never noticed when Jess had returned. It wasn't until hours later that he stopped to stretch and realized that Jess was intent on his own work across the room.

Chuck wandered over to Jess, who swiveled around in his chair. "Ready to talk some more?" Jess asked with a welcoming grin.

Chuck hesitated for a moment; he hadn't actually planned this. But he had thought of a few things, so he pulled up a chair and pulled out some paper. "I was thinking, it's all about time," he said.

Jess raised an eyebrow. "Hmm?"

Chuck took a scrap of paper and drew a horizontal line.

"Look, if this is a timeline, we're here." He put an x on the line. "We're at a certain level of efficiency. But up here-" he drew another horizontal line a few inches above the first, "for competitive and myriad other reasons, we need to be working at this level. The only issue is trying to quickly get from this level to the other."

Chuck blinked at the paper as the idea he'd had with it fizzled and died. "I forget how that was supposed to be helpful," he admitted ruefully.

But his initial explanation had sparked an idea in Jess. "No, look at this, mate," he said, pulling the paper toward himself. "What if this wasn't a timeline, but a graph?" He labeled the x-axis "time" and added a y-axis labeled efficiency." "Now say we're at point x-" he marked it near the origin "-and we want to get to y." He placed the second point on the top line and to the right of the first.

"So?" Chuck asked.

"So we have two ways to get there," Jess said, his voice sounding much more alert and excited now. "The old-fashioned way, developing solutions in sort of a vacuum for a long time and then in a short period of time throwing out all the solutions onto the users." He drew a horizontal line across from the lower point till it was equivalent to the upper point, then he drew a vertical line to the second point. "It's how we do it, and it is not the shortest distance.

Or the new way, with continuous change." This time, he connected the two points with a diagonal line. "Which is better?"

Chuck stared at the diagram. "The shortest distance between two points..." he gasped.

"Is a straight line!" Jess beamed. "Hey, that reminds me of construction."

"Huh?"

Jess shrugged. "They've got the construction going again on the freeway, you know. I was just complaining about how if they do constant maintenance—sure, it's annoying to have the roads shut down once in a while, but it's only for short periods of time and in the off-hours. But if they let it go, like they usually do, for years, we drive on nice roads for a short while, bad roads for a long time, and then they have to close the whole road for months to get it back into shape. That's exactly how our implementations work."

Chuck smiled. "That's exactly how it is! That's a great analogy, much better than mine."

"What was yours?"

"Well, it seems to me that it's like exercise. You have to do a little every day. If you don't work out and then try to do all the weights and machines for eight hours straight one day, you don't actually end up getting in shape—just sore."

Jess nodded. "Good point. Especially if you think about those athletes—you know, ones like me—who do great while they're in organized sports and their coaches push them, but turn into fat, lazy couch potatoes as soon as they don't have a routine anymore."

Chuck looked critically at his friend's waistband. "You don't look like you're getting too fat, you know."

Jess punched him on the shoulder. "That's not what I meant and you know it."

"Anyway," Chuck continued, "the point is that we need a transition that takes place over time—not one big jump all at once. And this project is the way to get it."

"So the company can constantly be changing and improving," Jess said, nodding in agreement. "Genius, mate!"

"Hey, by the way, it actually won't be a straight line," Chuck added. "It will be tiny stair steps." He pulled the drawing over to him. "Hmmm. I wonder if there is a theoretical way to compare the efficiency of a shorter process to the area under the curve. Oh, sure if you calculate the area of the large triangle, you can call the value the amount of opportunity lost, or should I say opportunity *cost*. Then, sum up the area of the little triangular stair steps. The comparison of the area, or opportunity cost, is something like 90 percent better if you take small steps—and that's not even considering how far off from the expected efficiency the old process gets you. Remember, small steps are inherently goal seeking since they can change direction based on feedback from the last little step."

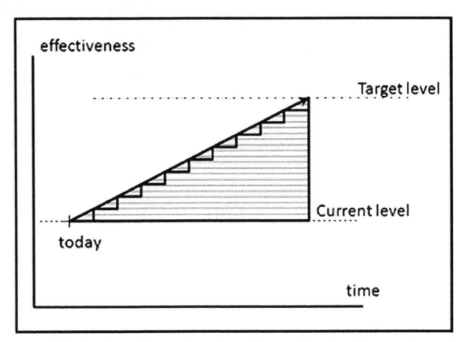

"That's going a bit too far, mate. You could make this your doctoral thesis and still have to work on Thanksgiving. Let's stick with the practical, okay? The handy point is that the vertical leg shows people are changing as well as technology. That is vital."

Just then, Chuck's desk phone began ringing, interrupting their impromptu strategy session. "Oh, well," Chuck grimaced, "back to work!"

9

"Dad! Will you help me with my Pinewood Derby car again tonight?"
"Sure, Ben. Just let me finish up here." Chuck opened the e-mail
from Jess without really thinking about it, assuming he was asking for help
on yet another glitch. He started to skim through it, but the message surprised him; he had to slow down and read it again.

"Hey, mate," the message read. "If you really want to go about changing the world, here're a few things you might want to consider. It'll cost more
to install software little by little; economies of scale and all that. And the
company's not going to want to pay for upgrades that often. Even if it didn't
cost more, who wants to be shelling out that kind of money every month
when you can do it every two years instead? Not that I don't like your idea,
you know. You just have to think about the economic side of things. Cheers!"

"Da-ad!" Ben appeared at his side, and by the sound of it, some serious
whining had been going on that he'd missed.

"All right, I'm coming." He glanced once more at the e-mail, but Ben
grabbed his arm and shook it.

"Come on, Dad!"

Chuck closed his laptop, trying to hide his sigh of regret. He forced a
smile as he turned to Ben. "Now, where were we?"

They'd carved the rough shape of a car over the last few weeks; now
they needed to attach the wheels. Chuck started measuring. "The directions
say they have to be the right width to fit on the track. Will you read them
to me again, Ben?"

"Can I measure, Dad?"

"Sure." But the boy held the car and tape measure so awkwardly that
Chuck had to intervene. "No, look, son. You have to get it perpendicular to
the edge if you're going to get it right. Here." He marked the point carefully
with pencil on the bottom of the car. "Now you try."

But Ben still struggled. Chuck checked his watch; he didn't have time
for this. Ben had to get to bed, and he had to finish his work. Finally, he had

42

to take the reins—doing the measuring and driving the nails himself, with Ben watching over his shoulder.

"Thanks, Dad," he said when Chuck handed him the finished assembly. Then he set it back up on his shelf and headed for the stairs.

Pensively, Chuck ran the car back and forth a few times. It rolled perfectly. Ben would be more excited when he got to paint it, he decided, and went upstairs to help Cathy get the children ready for bed.

***

It wasn't until midmorning the next day that he could corner Jess. "I got your e-mail," he announced as soon as Tony stepped out of the room.

Jess just raised an eyebrow in silent query.

"What were you talking about with that economies-of-scale stuff?" He'd been racking his brains about it; it sounded vaguely familiar, but he couldn't think what it meant in this context.

"It's quite simple, lad," Jess said, gesturing grandiosely with his coffee cup. "Companies only have to pay once when they install a new product all at once. All the major suppliers give them discounts when they buy a lot at once. One set of hardware, one installation, and one set of software training costs significantly less than adding all those things in every time you want to change a little niggling detail."

"Okay," Chuck said slowly. "That's about what I'd thought. But..." He thought about the bundles Nathan was trying to buy and all the useless applications in them.

When he didn't continue, Jess grimaced and said, "But what? Come on, spit it out."

"Well, you're right that it's cheaper to install lots of things at once—except that no one ever uses all the things they install. We lose just as much money by piling things up to use later that end up being useless." Chuck wasn't exactly sure how to articulate what he was thinking; he looked up at Jess hopefully.

Jess frowned. "I'm not sure I follow you."

Chuck tried another angle. "Look, you know how many licenses Purchasing gets for us a year?"

"I couldn't give you a number, but too many should be a rough guesstimate."

"Exactly. And how many do we actually use?"

Jess ticked a few off on his fingers. "Maybe a dozen."

"Right. The way I see it, they only buy all those titles because they think we might need them. But by the time we get around to doing an annual or quarterly upgrade, they're already obsolete and we have to buy new ones anyway."

Jess was still frowning. "But we still wouldn't save any money by doing it more often. We'd just install the one and use it a little before it became obsolete, but then we'd have to install another just as soon."

"So we'd be using all the licenses we bought. That's a lot less wasted money."

But Jess was still shaking his head. "Besides, the whole point is to find an upgrade that will still be good for a long time, so that we don't have that issue. Sure, it's not perfect, but the idea is that if we pay the money for the best technology now, we won't have to change things around for several years."

"Yeah, you mentioned that in the e-mail, too, but that doesn't make sense. When have we ever been on the cutting edge of technology?"

Jess laughed. "Hey, every time that the program doesn't work properly, isn't that because it's on the cutting edge and hasn't had time to work out the bugs?"

Chuck shrugged. "It still seems to me that we should be able to respond more quickly to technological changes."

"Well, obviously that's the only way to survive in business nowadays," Jess said, taking another sip of coffee. "But this company is just too big and has too much momentum to be able to turn on a dime. That's why small companies are the ones that respond properly to new technology. We're always the last to get it."

"So don't you see?" Chuck leaned forward. "With this new system, we would be on the cutting edge. With one team constantly managing technological changes, we'd never be playing catch-up. The company would be far more competitive! That would surely outweigh the extra cost of upgrading more often."

Jess stared at him for a long moment. "You're really serious about this, aren't you?"

Chuck nodded, a little surprised himself. "Yes, I guess I am."

"Well," Jess said as he leaned back, "I'll keep bouncing ideas around with you, if you like. If a great innovation is going to come out of this, I want my name to be on it."

"Sounds fair to me!" Chuck grinned. "So, what do you-"

"Well," Jess repeated, "the problem with flexibility is that it blows away the standard processes."

"What?" Chuck frowned.

"Look, we have to have standard business practices, right? They have to be documented and we have to be following them to be certified," Jess explained. "The problem is that flexibility and standard are mutually exclusive terms—two conflicting constraints in the lingo of the laws of innovation. So we need to exploit the constraint, as so aptly taught in *The Goal*, right?"

"Right."

"Consider the constraint of the standard business practices or operating instructions," Jess said. "What has to be done to exploit them? We need to update them each time we upgrade the applications...heads up." Chuck swiveled around to see Tony approaching the door. He turned back to his own computer.

"Things going all right?" he heard Tony ask behind him.

"No problems," Jess said lightly. "Or, at least, no new problems."

"Good, good," Tony replied. Chuck got his e-mail open and saw a list of new e-mails from the user group. He clenched his teeth to keep back a sigh and opened the first one.

10

Somewhat to his surprise, Chuck was not the first in the office the next morning. "Hello, Susie."

"Morning." Susie glanced up and smiled, but quickly turned back to her computer screen. "How are you?"

Chuck started arranging his things on his desk. "Fine. You?"

"Mmm. Hey, what's that stuff all about?" Susie didn't look up from the screen but jerked her head toward the whiteboard in the back of the room. Chuck looked at it, surprised. That whiteboard held week-old notes and scribbles and conversations; one of these days, they'd get around to erasing the oldest stuff, but for now, there was still some space left.

He hadn't really looked at it as he came in. Now he saw that it wasn't nearly as much space as there had been the day before. At the top of the new sets of scribbles was his name, done in multicolored caps with dots of color all around it. Obviously Jess's work.

What could he tell Susie about it, though? "It's just some stuff Jess and I were talking about," he said as casually as he could. "I hadn't noticed that he'd gotten back to me. Thanks; I'll go read that now."

"You guys are spending a lot of time on that." Was that a faint accusatory note in her voice? "Do you think we'll have the upgrade ready on time?"

"Sure we will." Chuck tried to sound confident. "We're just playing around with the idea now and then. We're getting all our work done." He fretted over the many details of the upgrade plan on which he had yet to start. If he didn't get that done soon...

"All right." Susie didn't sound convinced, but Chuck didn't linger. He went over to the whiteboard, trying to position himself so that he didn't block the doorway entirely, leaning back against the conference table as he tried to decipher Jess's scribbles. "Why can't he write like a normal person?" he wondered aloud as he turned his head to the side to follow a line that ran perpendicular to the floor.

The message ran, "Hey, mate. If you really want to do this, you've got [illegible scribble] think about. How are you going to get stuff certified with this new system? Can't just have new software and business processes running amuck—anarchy, like I said. [Another scribble.] Cheers!"

Chuck grabbed the eraser and wiped the whole thing, lost in thought. He knew it wouldn't have to be anarchic; he just had to figure out how to do it.

"Hey!" A hand grabbed his wrist. "I still need that!"

Chuck looked from the board to Jon's scowl, where he'd gone from erasing Jess' message to erasing the remainder. "Ooops, sorry," he said sheepishly. "I wasn't thinking."

"That was obvious," Jon said, pushing past him to restore the missing lines. "At least you got that garbage of Jess's out of the way. He just takes up the whole board."

Chuck edged away and made a discreet retreat.

***

Chuck was answering some users' e-mails when Jess tapped him on the shoulder. "I didn't scare you off with that easy question, did I?" he asked, sitting back on the central table as Chuck turned to face him.

Chuck blinked at him, then glanced back at the whiteboard. "Oh! I haven't had time to think about it." His eyes narrowed. "Wait, what makes you say it was easy?"

Jess smiled smugly. "Oh, you know, you pose a question, start thinking about possible answers and counters you can make to them…"

"So you have a solution?"

"Sure, don't you?" He laughed outright at Chuck's expression. "All right, all right. We have to do testing on everything we buy, sure. But the best way to do testing is in parallel! We all know that when the users actually do their work on the new system, we find out about all kinds of problems that never came up in those 'use case scenarios.' " He spoke the last phrase with distaste. "Anyway, if we did make small incremental changes, the users could test the new system in parallel with the old one, and we'd be right there to fix any issues."

"By the time testing was done, we'd know it worked," Chuck said slowly. "We wouldn't be expected to move on after testing use cases and have to figure out the users' problems while working on the new project." He grinned. "That's brilliant, Jess!"

"I know I am," Jess said with a grin. Then he leaned closer, conspiratorially. "You have a pretty good idea there, y'know. While Tony's out, what say we try to iron a few more of the wrinkles out?"

Chuck glanced back at his computer, an imperious summons to the work he should be doing. But the siren call of this new idea was harder to resist. He turned back to Jess. "Why not?"

"All right!" Jess cheered. "Let's make a list of all the problems this thing will solve." He moved to the brainstorming whiteboard at the rear of the room. "First of all, we'll let the users define the requirements, instead of letting people who don't know anything about the project do it." He wrote as he spoke, a quick green scrawl.

Chuck stepped up beside him and grabbed the blue marker. "We won't have all those unused licenses lying around; we'll only buy the ones we need."

Jess tossed his marker up in the air and caught it deftly. "We won't lag so far behind technology," he added to their list.

"And we'll do testing in parallel," Chuck continued. He stepped back and surveyed their list. "It's a pretty good start."

"I'd say so," Jess said. He started adding stars and dots around their list. "We should show it to Tony."

"This?" Chuck looked incredulously between Jess and the whiteboard.

Jess laughed. "No, we'll have to make a presentation. But he should know what a good idea we have."

"We? I came up with it."

"Yes, but without me, would you ever have gotten it to Tony?" Jess smiled when Chuck struggled for a reply. "See? We."

"All right," Chuck agreed. "But how do we think he'll buy into this?"

"The more apt question is, how will everyone else buy into this? Tony's going to make his decision based on what his peers would think of it, after all."

Chuck frowned. "Well, we aren't going to talk to all of them."

"No, we have to tell Tony what he could say to them that would convince them that he's onto something great and not off his rocker." Jess looked at Chuck quizzically. "Haven't you ever thought about this, mate?"

"I try to stay as far from management muddles as I can, thanks," Chuck said, turning back to the board and setting his marker down.

"Why? Management is where it's at!" Chuck stared at Jess, but for once he didn't seem to be joking. "Come on, Chuck! Where else can you know what's actually going on and get the money for what you know, rather than the drudge work we're left with? I'll be there someday."

Chuck shook his head, surprised that he never realized that Jess had such ambitions. "Well, then, manager-to-be, how do we convince Tony that this might work?"

Jess drummed his fingers against the eraser tray. "Well, let's see. The whole point of this new system is that it works on very small steps. So all we have to do is convince a few people to try it and show them all these benefits." He waved a hand at the whiteboard. "User testimonials will carry the day, if we do our jobs right."

Chuck grabbed a chair from the central conference table and sat, staring at the list they'd created. "Like a grassroots effect."

"Exactly. It's really the most effective change vehicle." Jess sounded smug.

"This new plan better be as brilliant as we're all thinking," Chuck observed, "or we'll never get beyond step one."

Jess refused to be dissuaded. "Oh, it will be," he insisted. "As soon as a few groups see how great it is, everyone will want it. And then, we'll take over the world! Bwah-hah-hah-hah!"

Chuck just stared at him.

Jess laughed. "Sorry, mate. Couldn't resist."

Chuck decided to change the subject. "I don't know much about management, but it seems to me that no one would want to use a new approach on their next project."

"Good point." Jess took his own chair and leaned back until it hit the table. "But I know there are people out there hungry for a chance to make a name for themselves. If we set it up so the risk takers would be given credit for the success…"

"I guess." Chuck shook himself and tore his gaze away from the board. "Do you really think we should show this to Tony?"

"Of course! It's a genius idea, mate. You ought to be excited to show it off." Jess met his gaze squarely, a hint of anticipation in his eyes. "You whip up a presentation, and I'll tell him we want to talk to him tomorrow."

"Tomorrow?" Chuck struggled to breathe. There was no way this was ready to show to Tony, and it wouldn't be ready the next day.

"Sure thing. It'll be great." Jess stood up and shoved the chair back under the table. "E-mail the presentation to me when you finish, so I can look it over, too." Without a backward glance, he walked back to his desk, leaving Chuck staring blankly after him.

11

Over lunch, Chuck finally got up the courage to open a new presentation. He stared at the title slide for a long time before he finally typed, "Shorter Implementation Cycles." As soon as he had the first slide done, some of the tension in his back eased, and he started to type faster.

He refused to let himself wonder whether he could actually convince Tony that this was a good idea. Right now, he just needed to get the words written down; then he would worry about being persuasive.

Chuck started to list all of the problems he and Jess had seen in the current system, starting with the fact that the current upgrade would do no good, both because it was out of date and it was not what the users wanted or needed. The clunky custom code they were wasting their time writing, the technology lag caused by the year it took to plan the upgrade, the unused licenses that hung around wasting their money—all of these would be solved by shortening the implementation cycle. *It would be great,* he thought.

Situation

· Problem—We can't get new software features out to users in a reasonable amount of time. The users continue to use less productive methods.

· Problem—We face difficulties working with software applications that are no longer well supported by software vendor. The support staff spends a disproportionate amount of time handling issues that have either been fixed or no longer exist in newer software versions.

· Problem—We find it difficult to keep support staff with special expertise on the team. For example, since requirements are captured only once per cycle (and since cycles don't occur that frequently), requirement specialists are difficult to engage.

· Problem—We use outdated license packages. Some unused licenses are being paid for and newer licenses aren't available for use.

· Problem—We are unable to quickly enable some software features, check to see whether they are used effectively, and change the configuration based on feedback.

Target

· Provide software features to users within a reasonable amount of time after the software's release.

· Refocus the support staff from backing work-arounds on old software to managing requirements and implementing game-changing technology.

· Create a level resource plan for a multi-expertise support staff to work on all aspects of the implementation—from requirement capture through development and testing to user training/support and issue resolution.

· Renegotiate license packages more frequently to remove unused and outdated features and to obtain access to new features.

· Monitor the use of new features, revise their configuration and redeploy based on feedback to achieve higher user productivity.

Proposal

· Reduce the software application implementation cycle by reducing the scope of implementations.

After he finished the rough draft of the presentation, he sat back, a silly grin on his face. *This idea is wonderful,* he thought. He couldn't remember the last time he'd been this excited about something to do with work. It was a nice feeling, he decided. Maybe if this idea was approved, he might feel this way more of the time.

But he had a lot more work to do before it would win approval. This was only the rough draft, after all. He leaned forward again and went back to the first slide.

"Hi, Chuck."

He twisted around to face his visitor, surprised to see Henrich there. "Hi, Henrich. I didn't know you were with us today."

Henrich grimaced. "I'm not, actually. I just had an hour free and decided to come see if you guys needed anything. But don't tell Tony; I'm trying not to be noticed."

Chuck nodded. "Sure thing." He turned back to his computer as Henrich walked by, but his focus was gone. It was after lunch; he could hear other voices in the hall. He needed to get back to what he was really supposed to be doing.

With a regretful sigh, he closed the presentation and went back to his e-mail.

***

As soon as he entered the garage door, Chuck dropped his briefcase and held out his arms. "I'm home!" he called. Felice was already running toward him, and he heard other feet on the stairs.

He spun Felice around, then set her down to hug Julie and Ben. Everyone was smiling, which was a wonder. "How are you kids?" he asked.

"Good." "Great!" "Happy."

Chuck laughed and tousled Felice's hair. "I'm glad you're happy, kiddo. Where's your mom?"

"She's changing Little Bob," Julie volunteered. "She'll be down in a second."

Chuck picked his briefcase up and set it carefully aside, where it wouldn't get knocked over by his rambunctious brood. "Maybe I'll go meet her," he said, heading for the stairs. The kids tagged along with him, all trying to talk at once. He caught mentions of science fairs and art projects, but he'd have to revisit that later.

He met Cathy at the door to their rooms with an embrace and a kiss. "Hello, beautiful."

"Hello, yourself," she said with a smile. "You're late tonight."

"Really?" He looked at the clock over her shoulder. "Traffic must have been bad on the way home; I left at the normal time."

Cathy raised an eyebrow. "You didn't notice the traffic? What were you doing on the way home?"

He took Little Bob into his arms. "Oh, just thinking. It was a busy day." He turned his attention to the baby. "How are ya, big guy?"

"Anything exciting happen?" Cathy asked, sliding past him to head for the stairs.

"Well..." He suddenly wasn't sure how much to tell her. He hadn't really talked about his work on her idea. And they had no idea what Tony would say; he didn't want to get her hopes up for nothing.

On the other hand, he was pretty excited about the idea. It was hard not to talk about it. And she had inspired it, after all; she had a right to know.

"Well, you know that idea you had, about doing the installation in little bits instead of all at once?" he said as he followed her down the stairs. Cathy looked back at him blankly. Then her eyes lit up, and she nodded.

"Sure, I remember now."

"So, I was thinking about that, and I started playing with the idea—you know, how it could really work, in real life. I started talking to Jess about it, just throwing ideas around, and he thinks it has potential. We're going to present the idea to Tony. Maybe it'll even get implemented!"

Chuck waited for Cathy's excited reaction—nothing. She simply opened the oven without a word to check on its contents. Uncertain, he pressed on.

"Of course, we don't know that he'll accept it, or the directors, for that matter," he said carefully. "But we're working on it. We might actually change things, and you came up with the idea!"

She smiled at him as she set the pan on the stovetop. "That's great, honey." But there was no special enthusiasm in her voice; it was as if he'd just told her about another aspect of work that didn't apply to her and that she didn't really care about. "Kids! Time to eat!"

He took the hot pads from her and carried the food over to the table, perplexed. He'd expected her to be excited.

But that mystery would have to wait for a while. The kids were all clamoring for attention.

"Algebra is perfectly impossible," Julie announced. "I don't know why we have to do it. It's stupid."

"Do you want some help with your homework after dinner?" Chuck asked her.

She looked trapped. "Um, I guess, if it doesn't take too long," she said. He had to smile.

"We get the right answer when we do it my way, don't we?"

She smiled at him patronizingly. "Yeah, Dad, but it takes so long and so much paper! I can do it by myself much faster."

"Just so long as you do it," Chuck warned. She shrugged that off.

"Hey, Dad!" Ben interrupted. "I got a hundred on my spelling test today!"

"Great job!" he said. "That's awesome, bud! Give me five."

Ben slapped his hand, and Chuck snatched it back and shook it. "Ouch! That hurt! You're too strong for me."

The kids laughed, as usual. They never got tired of that joke.

Chuck turned to Felice.

"How's school going for you?"

"Great!" Felice slid off his chair and ran over to the refrigerator. "Look what I drew!"

Chuck took the picture and examined it admiringly. "What an amazing dinosaur! I love the colors!"

Felice beamed. Chuck was grateful that her drawing skills had advanced to the point that the images were recognizable. It was always embarrassing when he had to ask.

"May I be excused?" Julie demanded. "I need to get online with Sara and ask her about math."

"What? You don't want my help, but you'll chat online with people about it?" Chuck asked, trying to look offended.

Julie rolled her eyes. "Daaad, she's in my class. Actually, there'll probably be a bunch of us on, and we can figure out the answers together."

Chuck nodded. "Math by democracy. Very wise. And sure to produce the right answer."

"It works," Julie said, aggrieved. "We all get better grades when we do it together."

"Online study groups," he said, shaking his head. "What a world we live in."

"May I be excused?" Ben said, jumping up just as Julie rose. He ran to the sink just before her to rinse his own plate.

"Hey! You little rat!" Julie yelled after him, elbowing him.

"Kids…" Chuck warned. Ben stuck his dish in the dishwasher and slipped out of the room before any parental wrath could descend on him. Julie muttered to herself as she rinsed her own plate, but Chuck decided to let it go.

"I'm done," Felice announced. "Thanks, Mom!"

Abandoned by the kids, Chuck looked at Cathy. She was looking tired.

"You make sure Julie does that math," she sighed, taking another serving of green beans. "I can't handle it."

"Sure, honey."

She looked up, meeting his eyes. "You've been helping a lot lately. Thanks." She fiddled with her fork. "But…no word about Thanksgiving?"

Chuck blinked. "I told you; we're working on a presentation. If it's accepted, I'll be home for Thanksgiving."

She sighed. "Oh."

"What?" he demanded, hurt by her perceived lack of faith. "Don't you think we can do it?"

A sad smile crossed her face. "It's not you, Chuck; it's Tony. Everything you say about him—I can't imagine him accepting a proposal like that."

Chuck couldn't think what to say. Her thoughts matched too well what he'd been thinking. But he had to keep some hope. He could still make it home for Thanksgiving.

He didn't want to fight with her, so he cleared his plate, rinsing it several times while he collected his thoughts. He could hear her behind him, putting leftovers in the fridge. He put his dish in the dishwasher and turned back to her.

"It might really happen this time, Cathy," he said. "I don't want to promise anything, but I really think we have to hope this will work. I really am trying to be home for the holiday, honey."

She smiled at him. "I know you are," she said.

He sighed. "I'll go help Julie."

When he reached the living room, she was already typing away. He glanced at the screen, but didn't understand most of the chatspeak that was up there. At the speed she was typing, he wouldn't be able to follow a word.

She glanced over her shoulder, and her eyes widened. "Dad! What are you doing here?"

"Just making sure your homework gets done." He sat on the couch, looking over at her. "Where is it?"

She rolled her eyes, and then pulled her math textbook and paper from her backpack. "We were just saying hi. Sarah's dad is getting her an iPod Touch for her birthday."

"Really?" He tried to place Sarah. "What's her last name?"

"Timplin. But I don't think you know her." Julie opened the book and scowled at the problems.

Chuck knew he shouldn't interrupt any gesture toward studying, but he saw an opportunity to win some points with her. "Would you like an iPod for Christmas?"

"I have an iPod, Dad," Julie said, not looking up from her book.

"You do?"

"You and Mom gave it to me last Christmas."

Chuck winced. He'd let Cathy do all the Christmas shopping the year before, having been busy with an upgrade then, too. He'd seen the presents as the kids unwrapped them and not before. "Oh, yeah. I remember now."

She gave him a look he couldn't identify, then turned back to the computer and typed something. Getting the answer, she picked up the pencil and wrote a figure in her notebook.

"Do you think you'll need any help, kiddo?" he asked her.

"I'm fine." She didn't look at him. "You can do your work."

That hurt more than not remembering what he'd given her for Christmas. Was that all she saw him doing? Probably, he had to admit. He sighed. "All right. I'll be here if you get stuck."

"Mm-hmm." She ignored him as he left the room.

12

Jess was the one who cornered Chuck the next day. "Well?"

"Well, what?" Chuck asked, fighting to keep a straight face.

Jess mimed a punch at him. "Don't give me that! How's the presentation coming?"

"Oh, well, you know..." Chuck said, trying to look uninterested.

"You didn't do anything?" Jess sounded outraged.

"Why not? You didn't either," Chuck countered.

Jess opened his mouth to respond, then laughed ruefully. "All right, that's true enough. But you're not like me, mate. I expected something."

Finally, Chuck let himself smile. "I've got something."

"What?" Jess threw up his hands. "You are impossible, you know that? Abso-bally-lutely impossible."

Chuck laughed as he pulled his laptop onto the central table and opened the presentation. "It's just a rough draft, you know."

"Chuck." Jess gave him a stern look. "You do realize that you put more work into your rough drafts than I do into many final products?"

Chuck laughed, a little self-consciously. "Well..."

"You need to ease up, mate." Jess shook his head. "But why should I think you'd start listening now? Show me what you've got."

Chuck ran through the presentation quickly. It was hard not to gloss over the points, since Jess was nodding as soon as each slide showed up, but he tried to explain things as he would to Tony. Even so, it didn't take long.

"Well?" he said when he reached the end.

Jess grinned. "It's wonderful! Well done, you."

"What do you think I should change?" Chuck asked, scrolling through the slides. "I thought it faltered a little about halfway through."

"Quit your nitpicking!" Jess rolled his eyes. "Come on, let's show it to the boss."

"What?" Chuck sat rigid, staring at Jess. "You can't be serious."

"Why not? It looked good to me."

"But, but-" Chuck searched for a logical objection. "But it's not ready!"

"Sure it is. Come on, he's in his office. Let's tell him what we've figured out!"

Before Chuck could protest, Jess picked up the laptop and headed for the door to Tony's office. Chuck followed numbly.

***

Tony looked up and smiled when they entered. "What can I do for you?" he asked.

"We have something to show you," Jess said, holding Chuck's laptop aloft.

Tony raised his eyebrows. "Oh? Is this scheme to get out of working on Thanksgiving that you've been spending all your time on?"

Chuck felt his face flush. "We haven't been-" he started to say defensively, but Jess cut him off.

"It's much more than that," he said smoothly. "Oh, sure, it may have started out with a desire to be home for the holiday, but it's grown. Having to do the upgrade over Thanksgiving just made it clear to us how much the current system is flawed. We thought about it, and we decided that shorter implementation cycles would solve any number of problems." He set the computer on Tony's desk and opened the slideshow again. "This new method would be much more responsive to changes in technology and to the users, and it would foster innovation, rather than hindering it."

Tony still looked skeptical, but he listened as Jess went over the presentation. Chuck could only sit and watch, feeling useless. Why had they ever thought that they could convince Tony? This was impossible.

Jess finished the presentation and flipped the computer shut. He grinned at Tony. "Well? What do you think?"

"It's an interesting idea," Tony said slowly, and Chuck held his breath. "I'll be the first to admit that the current system does have flaws, but change isn't easy. What makes you think that this would catch on?"

Jess hesitated and glanced at Chuck.

"Well." Chuck licked his lips and tried to organize his thoughts. "The users would love it." As he spoke, his confidence grew. "Rather than waiting for the next scheduled upgrade to see the changes they're waiting for, they can have them almost as soon as they suggest them. It's their needs we're trying to meet, after all."

Tony nodded thoughtfully. "True enough. But how would you get the managers on board?"

Jess took that one, to Chuck's relief. "You make a good point. Getting the managers to let us take their system down and install stuff that may break and that forces them to retrain their users has been quite a challenge. In fact, I need to add that to my list of issues we face. But we are expecting both the installation time and risks going down significantly if we do smaller upgrades." He gestured at the computer. "They won't have to worry so much about the risks; they just work with us on agreeing to priority features to go into each little upgrade and then take the credit when their productivity increases." Tony leaned forward, but Jess kept going. "It's perfect for small projects! As soon as we've done one, everyone will see what good results we have, and they'll be queuing up to sign on."

Tony smiled. "That would certainly be nice." His gaze shifted away from them, and he drummed his fingers thoughtfully on the table for a minute. "Well, I can certainly understand your concept, but this presentation doesn't really do it justice." Tony turned back to them. "It sounds more like a list of complaints than anything else. You need to show how your idea will be the solution, rather than just listing the problems."

Jess nodded. "Sure, we could do that."

Chuck glanced at him quizzically. 'We?' he wanted to ask, although not in front of Tony. He didn't want to go back through the whole thing and change the way it was written.

But Jess was still talking. "Then can we show it to the director?"

The director! Chuck's heart sank. What was Jess getting them into?

"Jess…" Tony gave a laugh that ended in a sigh, shaking his head. "You're not going to leave me alone until you get what you want, are you?"

Jess just grinned at him again.

"All right, fine. Make it a proposal, and I'll send it to Kent. But I don't want to see you neglecting your work!" His voice was stern. "This is a fun idea, and it might get used later, but realistically, there's almost no chance that it will get implemented in time to overtake our current project. That has first priority."

"Sir, yes, sir!" Jess gave a mock salute, and Tony rolled his eyes at him.

"Dismissed!" he said, and Chuck was grateful to grab his computer and follow Jess out.

Jess walked straight through the room and into the hall; Chuck followed him without really thinking about it. They ended up in the break room, where Chuck sank into a chair and rested his head on his arms. He watched Jess pour himself a cup of coffee, leaning his head back to gulp it down. He sat down and grinned at Chuck.

"Not bad, eh, mate?"

"Not bad!" It came out as a croak. Chuck cleared his throat and tried again. "Are you crazy?"

Jess straightened up, looking wary. "What do you mean? Tony liked it! He said we could show it to the director."

"Exactly!" Chuck shook his head at his friend's lack of perception. "Jess, this is nowhere near ready to show to the director! We have to redo the whole thing, Tony said, and even so, it's hardly had the kind of work put into it that it needs to-"

Jess cut him off with an upraised hand. "All right, all right! I forgot who I was talking to."

"What's that supposed to mean?"

"Guess." Jess' grin was devilish, and Chuck shook his head.

"Never mind. How do you think we're supposed to get this into shape to show the director? Without neglecting our other work?"

"She'll be all right," Jess said, taking another drink of the coffee. "No worries."

"No worries?"

"Look, mate," Jess said as he leaned forward. "Don't worry about it today, all right? Tomorrow, we'll go to lunch together and talk about it. It won't take long to whip it into shape." Jess raised his hand to reassure Chuck before he could mount further protest. "Trust me, it'll be fine. We'll eat and talk and have it done in no time. I know a great Indian joint just down the street. Sound good?"

Chuck took a couple of slow breaths. When they couldn't get it done on one lunch break, Jess would see. They'd call off this whole idea about sharing the idea with the director. "All right."

"Atta boy!" Jess stood up. "Well, we'd better get back to work before Tony gets on us."

"Yeah," Chuck said glumly. He picked up his laptop and headed for the office.

13

Chuck firmly put aside any thoughts of shorter implementation until lunch the next day. He had to meet with the user groups and help them through the testing process. The next morning, Jon came to him with a terrible problem; it took the whole morning to sort out just what had gone wrong and get Henrich's help to fix it. They eventually found that on some of the data, a key attribute value was blank and caused the indexer to fail. They weren't able to figure out how the users had managed to create the data without the attribute, so the best they could do was to add code to handle the issue. Chuck added this issue to his list of things to look into when he got some time to spend with users again.

In fact, with all the distractions, he almost forgot about his lunch plans. He was wearily trying to get a little of his own work after finally getting Jon's emergency sorted out when Jess approached.

"Aren't you ready to go, mate?"

Chuck looked away from the screen, trying to remember what he was talking about. Then it hit him. "Oh, man," he groaned, not wanting yet another issue to tackle. He squeezed his eyes shut for a moment, trying to ignore the neon lines and falling dots on the insides of his eyelids.

"Come on. It'll be better than whatever you've been working on all day. I can tell that just by looking at you."

Chuck cracked one eye open. "Where were you when we were trying to fix those issues?"

"Getting my own work done," Jess said smugly. "I've got better things to do that run around putting out fires."

Chuck shook his head but got to his feet. "I don't think I'm going to be up to much," he confessed.

"Aw, all you need is some good curry," Jess said, leading him out of the room. "I'll drive, if you want," he added over his shoulder. Chuck nodded gratefully.

The bright sunlight hurt his eyes as they made their way through the parking lot, and Chuck shaded his face with his hand. What was the sun doing so bright in November? Not that he minded, but it didn't seem like winter.

They arrived at the Indian restaurant in record time. Chuck avoided looking at the speedometer of Jess's sports car; it was none of his business if his friend disregarded the speed limit. Jess walked in like he owned the place; the boy working the host stand smiled at the sight of him. "Mr. Albergard! We'll have your order ready in a moment."

"Actually, Audish, my friend and I will be eating in today, if you have a table."

"Of course!"

As the boy led them to an empty table against one wall, Chuck glanced at Jess. "Just how often do you come here, anyway?"

Jess grinned. "I like good food. What can I say?"

"I'll expect the best, then." Chuck unfolded the menu and stared at the dishes. "What is this stuff?"

"Don't you eat Indian, mate? Best food in the world!" Jess led him through the menu with careful explanations of the different spices and vegetables involved. Chuck finally ordered a mild dish; Jess went with something he'd described as "hot enough to blow your ears off."

After the waiter retrieved their menus, Chuck pulled out a pad of paper and a couple of pens. "Where should we start?"

"After we eat?" At Chuck's look, Jess held up his hands. "No, no. I retract the statement."

Chuck snorted. "This was your idea, remember."

"I just hate to ruin a good ambiance." Jess gestured around at the dark red fabrics and bright golden statuettes lining the walls. He looked down at the paper. "What have you got so far?"

"Got so far?" Chuck raised his eyebrows. "I've got nothing. You said not to worry about it, remember?"

"You're not going to make me do all the work?" Jess could sound truly piteous when he put his mind to it.

Chuck scrawled "Shorter Implementation Cycles" across the top of the paper and shoved the pad to Jess.

Jess stared back at him. "What? Is that all you've got?"

"This was your idea." Chuck knew he was being rude, but he really didn't want to be involved in this. Especially if it led to sharing this idea with the director.

"It's just what we said in the presentation. We just have to phrase it positively." Jess leaned over and grabbed the pen from him. "Reduce custom code by using the most recent vendor functionality," he wrote. "See? Now we say we'll be able to implement faster, which will allow us to use the fancy new options that are being produced, rather than hanging around in the dark ages." He tossed the pen back to Chuck. "Your turn."

Chuck tried to think back over the past week. That documentation process the consultants were working on...He grabbed the paper and wrote, "Only document the actual processes used to accurately represent the true workflow."

Jess read it and snorted. "That'll be the day."

"If we're changing in small steps and testing in parallel, it will happen," Chuck said. He smiled as he considered the implications. "Every time the users find a better way to do something, with all this new functionality, they'll want to tell everyone. Those process documents will actually be useful for once."

"You don't think small, do you?" Jess replied, still unconvinced.

Chuck rolled the pen back to him. "Here, it's your turn again."

Jess didn't even stop to think. "Process documentation will be relevant, sharing best practices between workgroups and divisions."

"Hey!" Chuck protested. "I just said that."

"Yes, but you didn't write it." Chuck shook his head at the smug expression on Jess's face. "Your turn again."

Chuck almost let the pen roll off the table as he tried to think. Enough about documentation, what else would this system do for them? The other major headache they always dealt with came to mind. "Do you think that this will help with data migration?" Even as he asked the question, he knew the answer. "Of course it will," he said before Jess could reply. "No more trying to figure out the perfect data model that could communicate with any system—we'll be focused on pulling data in as it's needed, when the users want it. Data migration will become part of the visible work process instead of a backroom batch job full of errors. It will conform to our mantra of self-correcting, short deployment cycles."

"What, you mean give up the search for the perfect data model?" Jess asked in mock horror. "But that's the Holy Grail!"

Chuck bent over the paper, which was looking a little ragged from being shoved back and forth. "Shorten feedback time when developing data migration methods by keeping current to user need." He tossed the pen to Jess, who caught it easily.

Jess twirled the pen between his fingers for a few seconds, looking over what they'd already written. Then he grinned. "The first thing you told me was that we buy too many licenses," he said, leaning forward to write a new entry. "Autocorrection of licenses (over and under use)."

Chuck grabbed paper and pen as another idea came to him. "Application of better software to support use cases," he scrawled across the bottom of the page, squeezing the last word in the corner.

"Looks like we need a new page," Jess commented. Just then, the waiter arrived with their meals. "Or not!" Jess tossed the pad back to Chuck, who fumbled it before hauling it in. "There you go!"

"Jess, I can put this into a proposal, but showing it to the director..."

Jess swallowed the mouthful he'd taken. "Don't worry about it, Chuck. Just make a proposal out of that-" he gestured to the pad of paper with his fork "-and we'll be in business!"

Chuck could tell that arguing wasn't going to get him anywhere. With a sigh, he picked up his own fork and started in on the meal. He coughed and nearly choked. Grabbing his beverage, he drank half of it in one gulp. He then stared at Jess, wide-eyed. "That was mild?"

Jess started laughing and didn't stop for almost five minutes.

14

As they finished dinner, Chuck looked across the table at Cathy. "I really have to get some work done tonight," he said apologetically.

She sighed heavily and started to clear the table. "All right."

"I'm sorry," he said feebly.

"I know. It's all right." She forced a smile before she walked to the sink, but her shoulders were still slumped. It only added to the guilt he felt.

He wished that he hadn't let Jess push him into writing the proposal. It seemed so stupid when he looked at it now. But he'd said that he would do it, so he had to. He pulled out his laptop and opened the proposal worksheet. That was the one good thing about this process. Jess had gotten a template from Tony for the proposal, so his job was just answering the questions. And he knew the answers. It was just a matter of typing them up.

"Dad! Will you play with me?"

"Not now, Felice," Chuck said without looking away from the computer.

"But Daddy…"

"Daddy's working, Felice. Go play with Ben, okay?"

"He doesn't want to play with me." Felice was a good pouter, Chuck had to admit. But the distraction forced him to delete an entire line.

"Then pick out the book we're going to read tonight, and I'll come when I'm done."

"Okay," Felice said with a long sigh. Chuck heard her trudge away.

***

Chuck kept half of his attention on the door the next morning. When Jess walked in, he pounced on him. "What did you think?"

"Eh?" Jess peered at him through bleary eyes.

Chuck gestured impatiently at the coffee cup and waited until Jess had taken a long drink. "The proposal. What did you think?"

"Oh." Jess blinked. "Good job."

"And?" Chuck made a circling motion with his hand, hoping to elicit some more feedback. He'd finally given up the night before and sent it to Jess with a plea to him to edit it.

"We'll see, I guess." Jess sat down at the long table and cradled his cup in his hands. "I sent it."

"You what?" Chuck didn't know whether to scream or cry. "To who?"

"I believe that's 'to whom'." Jess corrected. "You blokes murder the Queen's English."

"Jess!"

"What? Oh. To Tony and the director, of course. That was the plan, after all."

Chuck raked his fingers through his hair, briefly considering the merits of grabbing some and pulling it out by the roots. That kind of thing worked for geniuses, after all. "Did you edit it at all?"

"Why? It looked good. Didn't need anything."

Chuck abruptly collapsed in a chair. Resting his forehead on his hands, he stared at the tabletop.

"We should hear back soon enough," Jess said, apparently oblivious to his distress. "I'll forward you the e-mail as soon as I get it." He took another long gulp of the coffee and stood. "Till then, I guess I should at least pretend to be working."

Chuck stood motionless for a long moment after Jess walked off. He should have known better than to send it to Jess. He should have guessed that this would happen. But whenever he thought of the director reading that the unedited proposal, his insides twisted.

"Are you all right?" Susie's voice, right beside him, made him jump and look up. She was looking worried. "You look like you're sick."

"No, I'm fine," he said, dredging up a smile from somewhere. "Just a little tired, that's all." He got to his feet. "I'd better get back to work."

Henrich caught his eye. "How'd it go?" he asked softly.

Chuck shrugged. "We'll know soon, I guess," was all he could say.

"Well, I'm rooting for you," Henrich offered. "But I'm going to sneak out while you're busy and work on another project. Try to keep him from noticing, will you?"

"No problem." Chuck reflected that it wasn't likely to be a problem; Tony could be single-minded when he was focusing on a project. That was in Henrich's favor today.

"Thanks," Henrich said, putting his laptop away as Chuck squeezed past his chair.

***

Just as Chuck reached Tony's door, he heard voices behind him. Turning, he saw Tony and Jess turning into the office, cups of coffee in their hands. Chuck glanced hurriedly at Henrich, who winced and reopened his computer in an attempt to look busy.

"Where are you going, Henrich?" Tony asked, his voice merely inquisitive, but with steely undertones.

"Oh, you know," Henrich said, turning around. "I've got some other stuff to do today; I can't always be here, you know."

"Will you be here tomorrow?" Tony demanded. "We'll need you."

"I'll have to check my schedule," Henrich stalled, closing the computer again quickly. "But I'll be able to give you some time, of course. I'm not sure when it'll be, but I'll be by. If you need me, just get the stuff together and I'll do it then."

"I really need that copy of your schedule," Tony pressed.

Henrich bent down to stow his laptop and didn't respond until he'd straightened. "I'll get it to you," he said. "But if you'll excuse me..."

Chuck managed to get through the morning by concentrating on anything but the proposal they'd submitted. He had to attend a user group meeting, a very intelligent bunch, which made it easier to keep his mind in the here-and-now. The meeting dragged on with a couple of very vocal users arguing for acceptance of their way of managing data as the "standard" approach. When it finally came to Chuck's opportunity to field questions, they didn't have as many questions as thinly veiled complaints, which he handled as best he could. When he finally got out, well after he was used to having lunch, he found that some of his enthusiasm for the new process had been restored. At least if it were implemented, they wouldn't have to deal with the same old problems that showed up in every upgrade.

When he finally made it back to his own desk, Jess was waiting for him with a scowl on his face. Chuck stopped abruptly at the sight of him, his heart dropping. "What happened?"

"Didn't you read the e-mail?"

Chuck sat at the center table and pulled out his computer. "I've been in a meeting since ten."

"And you didn't check your e-mail once?" Jess pulled up a chair beside him.

Chuck managed a faint smile. "I was leading the meeting," he said tartly as he opened his e-mail.

"So?"

At least Jess still had some sense of humor. Chuck took a deep breath as he opened the e-mail Tony had forwarded them from Kent Frye. At least he knew in advance it was bad news, instead of anticipating.

The e-mail was short: "Tony, keep your team on task. This would never work. Leave off the wishful thinking and get the upgrade in place." Chuck read it twice before he realized that he was grinding his teeth. He consciously relaxed his jaw.

"Well," he said after a moment's pause, "I guess I kind of expected it."

"Expected it?" Jess glared at him. "It was a great idea! He should have been able to see that."

Chuck sighed. "Well, he didn't. So that's that."

"What?" Jess was still glaring. "You're not giving up that easily?"

"What else can we do? It's over." Chuck gestured at the screen.

"Over? It's not over till the fat lady sings, and she's not even warming up yet," Jess said. "Never work? Of course it would work. It's obvious."

"Obvious to us, maybe, but clearly it wasn't obvious to him," Chuck said. "Let's just let it go, Jess."

"If he'd only give us a chance…" Now Jess was grinding his teeth. "I'm not giving up!"

"What do you plan to do?" Chuck asked warily. He'd had enough of Jess's hare-brained schemes for the moment.

"Do?" Jess's grin was wolfish. "I'm going to keep talking about it, of course. And see if we can't come up with a way to show that fussbudget what we can do if we set our minds to it."

Chuck stood up. As far as he was concerned, the project was over. "I'd better get back to work."

15

He should have known, Chuck reflected, that he wouldn't get away that easily. Jess kept after him with questions, comments, and new insights into their idea. And he couldn't keep from joining in the discussions; they were too interesting. The new process—they had dubbed it "progressive steps," referring to the diagram they'd made the first time they'd discussed it—was a great one. If only someone else knew that.

Despite the fun he was having, he kept worrying. He tried to keep their conversations to a minimum—coffee breaks, lunch time, a few minutes here and there—but he knew that Tony had noticed. He'd taken to ostentatiously closing his door every time they started talking about it. Jess shrugged it off, but Chuck couldn't stop feeling guilty for wasting work time on something they'd been officially told to put aside.

Despite all that, Chuck found himself whistling on his way into the office. How long had it been since he'd last felt good about going to work? He couldn't remember offhand and decided not to try. He'd like to keep this good mood.

"Hey, Chuck."

He turned around to see Raj standing behind him. "Oh, hi, Raj. I didn't realize that you were here already."

Raj didn't show any sign of leaving, which was unusual. Normally, he wanted to get all the work he could done first thing in the morning.

"Well, how's it going?" Chuck asked awkwardly, wondering what was up.

"Tony asked me to talk to you," was the unexpected reply. Chuck blinked and looked down, and then up, as though the motion would help him figure out what Tony wanted Raj to tell them. He'd been half-expecting Tony to tell them off and make them get back to work, but it seemed odd to send Raj to do that. Tony had no problem doing his own dirty work.

"Really? What about?"

Raj gestured at the whiteboard, still full of their scribbles. "This. He wants me to help you make it work."

Chuck just stared at him. Then he snorted. "Seriously? You must be joking."

Raj shook his head. Then he smiled. "Well, he wants me either to make it work or to tell you to stop wasting his time."

Chuck nodded. "That sounds like Tony." Then the implications began to sink through to him. "Wait, really? You're going to help us with this? That's awesome!" He felt a grin broadening. "Wait till we tell Jess! I can't wait to see his face!"

"Yes, well, we could wait, but I'd just as soon have you start explaining this to me." Raj looked at the board with evident bewilderment. "I tried to follow your notes, but I just couldn't keep track of things."

Chuck laughed. "Sorry, we don't always put up complete thoughts. But sure, I can explain it to you. Have a seat."

He pulled out a chair with an extravagant gesture. Enthusiasm was filling him like a reservoir. He loved this idea, but he hadn't completely believed that it would go anywhere. But if Tony was sending Raj—well, that meant that there was hope for their plan.

"Wait a second," he said suddenly, and hurried back to his desk. Pulling out a pad of scratch paper and the new set of whiteboard markers he'd bought the night before, he came back to the end of the conference table. He laid the paper between them and took a pen from his pocket. "All right, here's what we've been thinking. We want a process that will allow us to shorten implementation times."

He paused, expecting an interruption, but he was used to Jess; Raj simply waited for him to go on. He cleared his throat. "Shorter implementation cycles will allow us to be more responsive to user requirements. We can implement a change quickly, see how it works, and then start the next thing that needs to be done, rather than saving up the changes to make them all at once. It will be much more adaptable."

Someone tapped the back of Chuck's head. He sat up abruptly from where he'd been hunched over the paper. Jess was staring at him.

"There's someone in my seat," Jess mock-whispered, looking askance at Raj.

Chuck grinned again. "Tony told Raj to help us with the project!"

Jess looked from him to Raj, then took a long gulp of coffee. "Am I still dreaming? Did you really say that the big man wants to help us with our project?"

"Either help you or put a stop to it," Raj explained again. "But I'm finding the idea fascinating. Do you really think it could save a company money?"

"Of course!" Chuck and Jess chorused. Chuck waved to Jess to continue.

Jess pulled out a chair and took another long drink as he sat. "Of course, it'd require a larger initial investment," he said. "So I still think it'd be hard to get the higher-ups to go along with it."

"But after the initial investment, it'd save a great deal," Chuck said, giving Jess a stern look not to torpedo the idea before they could sell it. "Just imagine it, Raj: software being configured and implemented based on suggestions from the users and upgraded frequently to reflect that change."

Jess harrumphed and pulled the pad of paper to him. "That's the theory; here's the practical," he said, getting out his own pen. "Look, if you assume a given amount for installation on the current method, divided by how long you use it, you've got the cost per month of the software. But with this new method, the software is being constantly updated, so it can be used much longer."

"And you save man-hours because it will actually do what the users need it to and change with them," Chuck added.

Raj laughingly raised his hands in the air. "All right, all right. I see the benefit. I did read your proposal, after all."

"Oh." Chuck deflated slightly at the mention of the ill-fated proposal. "Well, what do you think we should do?"

"You have a very nice idea," Raj said slowly, "and it does promise a lot of benefits. But how do you intend to make those happen?"

Chuck looked at Jess; he looked as blank as Chuck felt.

"By shortening the implementation cycles," Jess said slowly, as if he thought Raj was having trouble understanding him.

"Yes, but how?" Now Raj was looking at them as if they were ignorant. "How exactly will shorter implementation cycles work? How do you decide what goes into the cycle? Who decides?" He broke off and shook his head. "Here, just answer me this: How does a cycle start?"

"Well, um," Chuck began, "there's a need, I suppose..."

Raj cut him off with a wave of one hand. "I have a better first question. How does an implementation cycle start under the current system?"

Jess took that one. "Someone in management decides we need this new software, or this upgrade, or whatever, and buys it for us."

"And then?" Raj prodded.

"They make up a list of requirements. Actually," Jess corrected himself, "they usually can't be bothered to make them up, so they let the software person come up with them. And then they give it to us and tell us to implement the new software and meet all the requirements."

"Exactly!" Raj smiled at them. "And that's the cause of all the problems you're worrying about, right?"

"Of course! The nonsensical..."

Raj cut Jess off before he could start ranting. "Well, how is your new system different?"

Chuck blinked. "We're not upgrading when new software comes available," he said slowly, recognizing for the first time just how much of a change they were really proposing. "We're upgrading when the users tell us they need it."

Raj took a new sheet of paper and wrote "User-driven change." "And how will they tell you they need it?"

"We're certainly not going to spend all our time going around collecting user gripes!" Jess exclaimed defiantly. "There's not money enough to pay me to do that."

"Maybe we should let the front-line support staff gather the complaints and send the most common ones on to us," Chuck suggested.

Jess brightened at that idea. "Yeah, that's their job."

Suddenly, Chuck remembered the way Julie did her homework online. He smiled. "We could have a web forum," he said with sudden enthusiasm, "where all the support staff could post their ideas. They could also comment on each other's ideas, so we could get feedback and improvement on the suggestions before we even started thinking about creating them."

Jess grinned. "Great idea! Forums can be powerful. We could have a way of marking their experience, so that more experienced people's ideas would be shot to the top of the to-do pile. We could run polls! It could even automatically summarize and prioritize the suggestions, based on who voted for which ones. Then all we'd have to do is read it and choose which make sense to apply."

"Can it really do all that?" Chuck reflected that maybe he'd better ask Julie what forums could do. This might come in handy.

"Sure can! Don't you use the Internet?"

"Not those kinds of sites. I leave that to my teenagers." Chuck shot Jess a withering look.

"That's me, young at heart," Jess said, undaunted. Chuck shook his head, smiling at his irrepressible friend.

Raj had been writing as they talked. Now he looked up. "Then what?"

"Well, when we get the results, we decide what to implement when. We lay out a plan for the first step." Chuck settled himself more comfortably in the chair. This looked like it would take a while.

"What do you mean by 'step'?" Raj interrupted.

"That's what we're calling each cycle. Because we're only dealing with one piece of the system at a time." Raj only nodded, so Chuck went on. "Then we figure out how to do it and implement it."

"How?"

Jess rolled his eyes. "How? The same way we always do, obviously. We get the requirements and implement them."

"So there's no other change between your system and the current one except for where you get the requirements?" Raj's question was soft and calm, but Jess still bristled.

"Isn't that enough?"

"I just want you to think about it." Raj said stoically. "What effects will starting with user requirements have on the system?"

Jess stood up abruptly, his chair spinning away from the table to bump into Chuck's desk.

"All right, I've had enough of the dum-dum questions," Jess said. "We know what we're talking about, even if you don't. I need more coffee. Then I'm getting to work." Jess stalked off without another word.

Chuck's gaze followed Jess then turned to Raj, who shrugged. "Sorry," Raj said, sounding more tired than apologetic. "That happens sometimes."

"Well, I need to think some more about your questions," Chuck said. "And Jess is right; we need to work on the current project."

Raj nodded silently.

"Maybe we could discuss it again tomorrow? If I have an answer for you by then?" Chuck suggested hopefully.

Raj's smile was friendly. "Of course! I'd like that."

Chuck realized uncomfortably that Jess's reaction really had hurt Raj. Unsure of what to do, he turned toward his desk. "Till tomorrow, then."

16

As he pulled into the driveway, Chuck felt the last of the day's stress release. He surveyed the yard as he stopped. The hedges needed to be trimmed again. Maybe he'd have some time to get to that over the weekend.

"I'm home!" His voice echoed depressingly; there was no scurry of feet or calling of greetings. Frowning, he set his briefcase down. What was going on?

Then he heard a soft giggle that someone was trying to hide, and he started to grin. "Oh, dear, I guess no one's home," he said loudly. "I wonder where they all went. I suppose I'll just have to go get pizza by myself."

No answer came, which was unusual for his kids. He turned toward the door, adding more bait. "And maybe I'll get some ice cream for dessert, even go see a movie if I want," he said, opening the door just as slight amount. "Too bad no one's here; they could have come with me."

Still no response. He stepped out the door and closed it behind him. For a moment, he wondered how mad Cathy would be, then brushed the thought aside and started the car. Whatever she'd made for dinner could wait. He headed out of the neighborhood to the nearest pizza place.

It only took ten minutes to get back with two pizzas. The smell was delicious. He couldn't understand how something so unhealthy smelled and tasted so good, but he loved it.

Opening the door with two pizza boxes in his arms was a little awkward. As he stepped inside, he caught a glimpse of someone running down the hall, back to a hiding place no doubt. He smiled and set the pizzas on the kitchen table.

He watched the clock, trying to guess how long it would be before the smell coaxed them out. But he wasn't patient enough for that, in the end. He opened the pepperoni box himself.

"Mmm, this pizza looks delicious," he said loudly, pulling out a slice. "If no one's here, I guess I'm going to have to eat it all by myself."

"Pizza!" Felice was, predictably, the first to break her silence and come running, grabbing him around the legs. "I want pizza!"

Chuck grinned down at him. "Oh, so I'm not here all alone! It's good to see you. Where's everyone else?"

Felice clambered onto a chair and reached for the box. "Hiding. I want pepperoni!"

Laughing, Chuck got out a stack of paper plates and served Felice a slice. "Coming right up! You and I get a whole pizza each, it looks like."

Finally, Ben and Julie came out, grinning crazily through an odd array of face paint. "Boo!"

Chuck gasped, clutched at his heart, staggered backwards, and finally slumped down dead. He stuck his tongue out for good measure.

Ben laughed. "We scared him to death! Mom, come see!"

Julie just stepped over him. "I want some pizza. Come on, Ben!"

As Ben stepped over him, Chuck surged upward, catching the boy in a bear hug. "Aaargh! I've got you now!"

Ben writhed, laughing helplessly as Chuck tickled him. "No! No!" he gasped between howls of mirth. "I want pizza!"

Finally Chuck let him up. "All right, go get your pizza," he said, pulling himself to his feet. He looked around. "Where's your mom?"

"Coming." No one looked up from the pizza. Chuck shrugged and went in search of Cathy himself.

He met her halfway up the stairs and stopped for a kiss. "Hello, beautiful."

She shook her head at him. "Pizza! I had dinner ready!"

"I know." He kissed her again. "But it's more fun this way. Besides, if you'd come out when I got home, I would have asked. But since there was no one here, I had to take matters into my own hands."

"Oh, so it's my fault, is it?"

He grinned. "Come on, you know whatever you made wasn't as good as pizza."

"What I made had vegetables and actual nutritive benefits," she said, trying to sound icy. But then she broke down in a laugh. "So, no, it wasn't as good as pizza."

"See?" He wrapped an arm around her and led her down the stairs. "Let's grab some before they eat it all."

They got seats at the end of the table as the kids finished their first slices. "So how was work?" Cathy asked as she plucked a slice.

Chuck swallowed hastily. "It was great! Tony had Raj come help us with our new implementation idea. It's making so much more sense now."

Cathy stared at him. "Really?"

"Yeah! I really think this is going to go somewhere, honey. No more doing huge upgrades over holidays!"

She smiled back at him. "Well, that's wonderful! Congratulations!" She must have noticed a shadow crossing his face, because she said quickly, "What's the matter?"

He forced the smile back. "Oh, nothing. It's just that Jess didn't like Raj's help much." He took another bite of pizza, but she didn't say anything. Awkwardly, he chewed and swallowed. "I'm sure it'll be fine. It's just hard—it'll take both of them to make this work, and if they're fighting, it won't be easy."

"May I be excused?" Ben and Julie spoke almost in unison, and then glared at each other.

"Yes, you may," Cathy said. "Be sure to wash your hands! Ben, finish your English homework before you get on the computer!" She had to raise her voice at the end as the kids scurried off. She turned back to him with a sigh. "I'm sure it'll work out, hon."

"Thanks." He finished the last of his crust. "Well, since I'm here, what do you want me to do? Help Ben?"

"Could you spend some time with Felice? She's been missing you."

Chuck winced, thinking of the way he'd brushed his daughter off the other night. "Of course I will."

***

Chuck paused outside the door to the office when he heard his name spoken inside.

"-are wasting time we need on this project! We'll never get it done if they don't buckle down!" That was Jon, his voice raised in anger.

"What does it matter?" Henrich sounded like he was only half paying attention. "If they want to waste their time, that's their business. As long as they're not asking me to sign on with them, I don't care what they do."

"Yes, well, you're not really part of this project, after all. Your employee review isn't riding on how well we do," Jon said. "But that's what you meant, isn't it, Susie?"

"I only said that I wondered how they would get everything done, with all these distractions," she snapped, sounding harried. "I don't know. Maybe they'll do it with no problem. But I'm a little worried sometimes."

Chuck realized with a start that he was eavesdropping. He straightened his shoulders and walked into the room.

The room fell abruptly silent. Susie was starting at her computer, but he could see the blush creeping up her cheeks. Henrich was lost in his computer, as well. But Jon was glaring at him belligerently.

"So, you're finally going to do some work with us," he said flatly. "Or are you off to discuss your own things again?"

"I was at a user's group meeting," Chuck said evenly, setting his bag down on his desk. "And Tony told Raj to discuss things with Jess and I. Talk to him if you have a problem with it."

He couldn't afford to get angry. He knew how Jon felt, like everything was falling apart and he didn't know how to fix it. He'd felt that way himself often enough, early in his career. Now, of course, he could fix things, and he did his best to help like the mentors who'd helped him. But Jon's defensive nature made it difficult. He opened his laptop.

To his relief, Jon returned his own desk. Chuck tried to forget what had just happened as he worked on his deployment plan, which was growing in complexity. The time required to complete the prerequisites was mushrooming beyond the time they had allocated.

He waited until lunchtime. When Jon and Susie had both left the room, he walked around the table and took a chair next to Jess.

"What's up?"

"Are we wasting our time on this?" Chuck asked softly.

Jess turned away from the computer and looked at him straight on. "What brought this on?"

Chuck didn't meet his stare. "I overheard some people saying that the team wasn't going to make the upgrade because we're not working enough on it."

"Jon?" When Chuck didn't answer, Jess smiled wryly. "Don't worry about him. He just likes to hear himself complain. Tony told Raj to help us! That means it's on the up-and-up."

"Yeah." Chuck couldn't muster much more enthusiasm.

"Not that Raj's help is good for much. Wasting our time with stupid questions!"

"They did help us explain what's different about our process," Chuck said. "I was thinking about it last night, and I came up with some more ideas."

Jess waved that aside. "Right, maybe, but it's still a pain."

"You will still help, won't you?" He hadn't meant it to sound quite so much like a plea.

Finally Jess smiled wryly. "Of course. It beats doing the stupid make-work Tony's assigned me." He muttered, "Even if it is ridiculous."

Chuck pretended that he hadn't heard the last. "Good! Then let's go talk to him."

"Now?" Jess moaned as he looked at the clock.

Chuck had to laugh. "To set up a time to discuss things this afternoon. We'll make sure it's after you get your takeout."

17

"So, what have you come up with?" Raj asked as Chuck and Jess settled themselves in his tiny office. It was more like a cubicle, but at least it had a door. Chuck realized that it probably wouldn't keep Jon from complaining, but if they were in another room, maybe he wouldn't realize what they were doing.

Chuck pulled out the notes he'd made. "We already talked about getting the requirements from the users. That means that once we decide which requirements need to be done, we need to present them to management for help setting a priority in support of the business plans."

Raj nodded. "Good."

"Then, we talked about making the decision to purchase new software; we need to decide if adding new software is required or the features are available in the old."

"Both," Jess said immediately. "We can decide whether new software, new functionality, or the current software works best for each requirement. We decide, not management."

Chuck jotted that down. "Sounds good. So then we talk to the users and end up with an agreement about what exactly needs to be done, and when."

"How is that different from what happens now?" Raj asked.

"The company assumes we need to get as much value out of the software 'investment' we've made, so it postpones upgrading until the software vendor threatens to charge us for support of old software. Then the company makes a mad dash to guess how many licenses will be needed and argues with the vendor about what kind of a deal they can give us. The whole contract is completed behind closed doors. Once the deal is finalized, we are assigned to 'roll-out' the software."

"All right. Then what?"

"Then we'd work with real users and find out what really happens," Jess muttered. Chuck shot him a quelling look.

"Then comes the part that's similar to what we're familiar with. We have to write up the requirement documents, do user testing, get formal approval, and implement it. Like Jess said, it'll be what we're used to, except in smaller pieces. We'll have to do it to get the hang of it." Chuck glanced at Jess, but he was still sitting in sullen silence.

"How will this affect testing?" Raj said.

Chuck hesitated. "Will it?" he asked, looking at Jess.

Jess only shrugged.

"Normally, we test whole systems to make sure they work in every scenario," Raj said patiently. "How can we test progressive steps?"

Jess snorted. "You know as well as we do. Why ask?"

"I may know better than you do." Raj was calm. Chuck didn't think he was trying to sound arrogant. "I want to know what you know."

Jess rolled his eyes. "Most of the benefit comes from solving only half the problems," he answered in a bored, sing-song drone. "After that, the returns diminish on each solution you implement. As long as we are solving a decent number of problems with each step, it doesn't matter if it hasn't been tested to see whether or not it helps some random scenario that only comes up once in a blue moon."

Chuck wrote as quickly as he could. That may have been obvious to Jess, but it wasn't to him.

"Nice." Raj nodded. "I'm just asking questions Tony or Kent will ask before this gets approved."

Jess folded his arms and leaned back in his chair. "Fine."

"And they will point out," Raj continued, "that the current culture supports large-scale IT projects. How can you start the opposite?"

Jess rolled his eyes. "Haven't we discussed this enough?"

Chuck ignored him and tried to think. "I don't think it matters," he said deliberately. "As long as we start somewhere, we can work in parallel to them. In the long run, people will see the benefit of smaller steps, and the culture will shift to our favor."

"Is that how you plan to deal with the lack of knowledge sharing?"

"Yep. As people see the success, they'll join in." He smiled at Jess. "Just like you've been saying: User testimonials are the way to go."

Jess snorted, but he looked a little less upset.

"You may have discussed it, but it didn't show up in the proposal," Raj said. "Neither did this point. How will these progressive steps line up with longer-term purchasing cycles and budgets?"

Chuck leaned forward before Jess could make another sarcastic comment. "Right, we did talk about that one. It will cost a little more up front, but in the long run, it will be better because we won't waste licenses or time spent looking for them. We'll only buy what we need when we need it."

Jess stood up abruptly. "I've had about all I can stand of questions you already know the answer to," he said sharply.

"Yes, our time is about up," Raj said, so smoothly that Chuck almost missed the flash of hurt in his eyes. "We'll talk more tomorrow. Until then, think about this: Your new approach all comes down to flexibility. How can we be flexible and standard at the same time?"

Without even replying, Jess walked out of the room as Chuck stepped aside awkwardly. "We'll think about it," he told Raj. "Thank you."

"You're welcome." Raj sounded distant, and Chuck left as quickly as possible.

He got quite a bit of work done that afternoon, toiling again to get the deployment setup steps as clear and crisp as possible, but through it all, he kept worrying about Jess and Raj. He had to make this work somehow, but it wasn't going to be easy.

He didn't speak to Jess for the rest of the day. But the next morning, he realized that he needed Jess's help getting the users' managers to set up the kickoff agenda. He paused a moment to stretch as he stood up before he walked over to Jess's desk.

"Hey, can you give me a hand? Talk to me about the kickoff meeting agenda. Will you call the manager and get them moving?"

As they finished, Chuck took a deep breath. "So, about that flexibility question."

Jess rolled his eyes in disdain, but Chuck pressed on.

"He's right, you know. There is a problem standardizing the system when we're going to be changing it so often. We have to follow standard business practices; we need to be certified."

"But," Jess said, picking up the counterargument in a bored tone, "we also need to be flexible to changes in market pressures and technology advancements. Without that, we're shooting ourselves in the foot; no one will admire our certification if it's based on software that's years out of date."

"Exactly," Chuck said. "So what do we do?"

"Hmm." Jess was finally considering the situation. "We'll buy certified software; that's not a problem."

"But how can we standardize the implementation system when each step could be so different?"

"That's it!" Jess whooped and held his hand out for a high five.

Chuck returned the gesture weakly. "What are you talking about?"

"A standardized system. Not the same thing every time, but a standard way to determine what we're going to do in each situation."

Chuck closed his eyes and ran through that last sentence again in his head. It didn't help. Opening his eyes, he held out his hands in supplication. "What are you talking about, Jess?"

Jess finally slowed down enough to explain things to him. "Look, businesses have to change to survive, right? Otherwise, they get so unwieldy and behind the times that they collapse. So what we want to do is manage that change. As long as we have a standard system—we define this process we're going to be using—we'll have traceability and standardization, but we'll be flexible enough to react to anything. Don't you see? Instead of having a lengthy, well-managed deployment project we'll have a well-managed—highly repeatable—deployment cycle. In fact, our process measurement targets will be in always meeting user needs instead of completing a project."

Chuck felt a smile spread across his face. "I see! That's perfect. We already took care of that."

"Yeah, no doubt Mr. Genius Boy saw that from the start," Jess said sarcastically.

Chuck rolled his eyes. "No, we thought of it, and it's a good idea! We came up with this idea, and we've made it into a really useful process. Raj just helped out a little."

"Some help." Then Jess straightened. "You really think it's ready?"

Reviewing what he said, Chuck wondered frantically what had given Jess that idea. "I just meant that we've made a lot of progress…"

But Jess wasn't listening to him any longer. "Perfect! Write up that new version for me, and I'll get it off!"

"When?" Chuck said sharply, trying to inject some sense back into this conversation. "I've got work to do today, you know. I'm busy!"

"You'll get it done," Jess said without missing a beat. "As you said, it's a great idea and a useful process. We've got it!"

Chuck decided not to argue. "All right, fine. I'll do the proposal when I get time." He wanted to add, "And then I'll wash my hands of it," but he couldn't. He still cared about this system too much.

Jess whooped again. Chuck found himself grinning back. It might take a while to get the proposal done, but at least the promise had made Jess happy again.

Later, though, he wondered if he'd done right to promise that so easily. Would he really be able to weave together a proposal based on just a handful of conversations? He started watching Raj's cubicle. He wouldn't interrupt him for something like this, but if he happened to come out…

It wasn't until Chuck was actually packing up to leave that Raj emerged. Seeing his opportunity, Chuck set his things aside and hurried over to him. "Hey, Raj!"

Raj glanced around, blinking as if the words had startled him out of some deep thought. When he saw Chuck, he smiled. "Chuck! What do you need?"

Chuck hesitated. "Jess and I figured out your standardization question," he stalled.

"Really?" Raj didn't give anything away, Chuck noted; his reply was simply quizzical, giving no hint as to whether he'd already formed an answer himself.

"Yes, we have to standardize this process, the one we're developing; it will be a standard process that allows the flexibility to rapidly change."

Raj was nodding before he got half the sentence out; that relieved Chuck.

"So, well, Jess—I mean, we were wondering if we were ready to write up the proposal, after all your help and everything." Chuck felt as awkward as when he was a teenager asking for a date.

Somewhat to his surprise, Raj didn't look offended. "He's ready to be rid of me, hmm?" he said lightly.

Chuck wondered how he could possibly answer that. "If you have more questions, that would be great, too," he said. "We've made a lot of progress since you started helping us."

Raj grimaced. "Thanks. And you're welcome."

Chuck waited for an answer, trying not to show that he was impatient. He found himself fiddling with his cell phone and quickly stowed it his pocket.

"Those were about all of the questions I had for you," Raj finally said. "I think you're about ready to rewrite the proposal, if that's what you want to do."

"Really?" Chuck felt his shoulders sag, and he wasn't sure whether it was relief at getting an answer or discouragement about the amount of work awaiting him. "I guess I should do that, then."

"I'd like to see a copy of it before you give it to Tony," Raj said casually. "That is, if Jess doesn't mind."

All traces of lightheartedness were gone from his face now. He looked like he didn't care, but Chuck suspected that Jess's attitude still bothered him.

"Of course he wouldn't mind!" It came out too loudly, and he tried not to betray how awkward he felt. "I'll get it to you," he said more quietly.

"Thanks." Raj continued out the door without another word. Chuck sighed. Things would just get worse if those two couldn't get along.

18

Chuck found it tougher to stay focused on the upgrade; the Progressive Steps project kept competing for his attention. He forced himself to spend the morning going through the testing results and preparing a management summary with appropriate conclusions. But over lunch, he pulled out his Progressive Steps notes and started looking them over. With Raj's help, they'd become an actual process document. It involved simple steps: Gather requirements from the front-line support staff, study how best to use software to support the requirements, discuss which requirements would be filled during the current step with the support staff, and then go through a formal document submittal, management approval, and upgrade process. Everything would be controlled and standardized by following the process, while retaining the flexibility to change by a quick feedback loop.

Unfortunately, by the time he had distilled those ideas from of his notes, lunch was over and it was time to get back to work. He needed more time to write the proposal. But when would he do it? He was risking getting behind on the real project already. Until their conversations with Raj, he and Jess were trying to avoid using too much work time to talk about this new idea. They had mostly done it at tail-ends of the day—as they came in or left for the day, right before or after lunch, or by leaving each other notes whenever they walked by the whiteboard, of course. Even Raj's questions had been quick. But this new proposal would take extended, intensive effort.

He'd have to do it at home. There was no other way to accomplish everything on his plate for today. Chuck sighed and put away the last of his lunch, his appetite but a memory. He'd planned to spend the evening with the kids. It was Ben's Pinewood Derby tonight. Well, maybe he could still go to that, as long as he worked the remainder of the evening. He could probably write when Ben wasn't actually participating in a race, after all.

Back at the office, the normally placid Susie was livid. One look at their workspace told Chuck all he needed to know. It had started raining again while they were at lunch, and the carpet was once again a sodden mess.

At least the desks escaped the deluge since none were directly beneath any windows.

"I don't know how long I can put up with this," Susie said, exasperated. "The smell is awful! How are we supposed to concentrate?"

Chuck shrugged. "I hadn't really noticed the smell, but...kind of like wet dog, isn't it?"

Susie wrinkled her nose in disgust. "Worse. Well, for me, at least; I like dogs. The only thing carpet's good for is keeping kids from dashing their brains out when they fall on it. Other than that, it's hardwood for me!"

Chuck had to laugh. "Well, we should be glad this isn't hardwood, or it'd be warping."

"You're probably right." She grimaced. "They should just tile this place like a pool and let it fill up. I'd rather go swimming anyway."

"Wouldn't we all?" He headed for his own desk, jumping over the tendril of water that reached all the way across the room. "If this rain keeps up, you might just get your wish."

"Keep thinking positive like that." The mirth in her voice made Chuck smile.

He sat down and was opening his laptop when he heard a hissing noise. Looking up, he saw that Susie had taken an aerosol can from her desk and was spraying its contents in the air.

"I really can't stand the smell," she said sheepishly.

Underlying the wet carpet odor, Chuck detected a faint floral scent.

"It's just a deodorizer," she said. "I thought it might help a little."

"Sure, I bet it will," Chuck said. Neither smell really bothered him, so he didn't care and turned back to his work.

But the question of that evening kept nagging at him. He had really wanted to be there for the kids. He couldn't work through Ben's Pinewood Derby. That would be like, well, like spraying an air deodorizer to get rid of the smell of wet carpets. He smiled to himself suddenly, struck by the parallel. That's exactly what he'd been doing. He was stinking up his family's lives by never being there for them, and then he tried to make it up with little superficial things like showing up at an event and doing work there instead of participating.

He started thinking about the vacation over winter break that he'd take with them. Then he looked down at the presentation, where he'd already noted the project's purpose—to shorten implementation times in order to make change constant in response to user needs.

He blinked as the idea suddenly seemed to apply to his own plan to go to Disneyland. He was planning a big change that would magically fix all their problems—except that it wouldn't. Maybe what his kids needed was constant bits of time and small changes that they wanted, not that he planned.

The ideas fell into place so clearly that he sat back in his chair, half-stunned. What was this? How could a work idea apply to his home life?

But even if it was just an analogy, it was a good one. He could feel it in his bones.

This would help.

And the first step was to implement it, right away. He had to go to the Pinewood Derby, eat dinner with the family, and read the kids a bedtime story. How was he going to do that?

He opened his planner and looked at the day. There just wasn't any free time.

"Trying to make more hours appear in a day?" Jon asked from behind him.

Chuck's attempt at a polite smile failed. "Yeah, I wish I could."

"Yeah, well, with this project, it's sure not going to happen anytime soon. This is ridiculous. Some of us used to have lives, until Tony decided to pre-empt them."

"You know what?" Chuck announced, coming to a sudden decision. "I'm going to make time for my life." He could almost hear Cathy cheering, as if she'd been there to hear his declaration. "I've got something to do this afternoon. If you need help with something, go ahead and ask, but I won't have those specs ready for you until tomorrow."

"What?" Jon said incredulously. He blinked a few times and stared, too taken aback even to hurl one of his patented barbs. "That doesn't sound like you, Chuck."

A slight smile stole across Chuck's face. "I know." He started to turn back to his work, and then peered up at Jon again. "You, uh, don't desperately need that stuff this afternoon, do you?"

"Oh, no, don't worry about me," Jon said, his sarcasm so obvious Chuck simply chose to ignore it. "It's not like I don't have fifty million other things to do today. Only about half of them depend on getting those specs, after all."

Chuck tuned him out. "Thanks, Jon." He turned back to his proposal. As he started to write, he found the ideas were flowing freely. Excitement overtook him once again. This proposal was going to be great! He just had to put the work into it to convince Tony.

He had to do some real work during the afternoon, but he stayed at his desk after everyone else had gone, continuing work on the proposal. He didn't want to leave it. At last, he stopped to stretch and looked at the clock. His eyes bulged in recognition of the time. He just barely had time to get to the Pinewood Derby if he left now!

He looked down at the proposal again, fighting the desire to push on. He was really on a roll—if he could just get that last bit filled out...

But there was no way he could do both, and he'd already decided to go to the Pinewood Derby. He threw his laptop into his briefcase and headed out.

19

Chuck put an arm around Cathy's shoulders as they settled into the stiff metal chairs. Ben was goofing around with the other boys down in the pit, but the other kids were sitting around them. He smiled to see them all together.

He reached out behind Cathy's back and tugged on Julie's hair. She broke out of her sulking to glare at him. "Dad! Cut it out!"

"Just want to make sure you're having fun, honey," he said.

Julie tossed her head in indignation. "Well, I'm not," she assured him.

He mimicked the head toss. "And you can't make me," he said in a high voice. "We'll just see about that." He reached over to tickle her.

She squealed and moved away, then straightened up to look down her nose at him. "Dad, please don't act like that," she said in a withering tone, as if his behavior was just too much to bear.

Feeling a little embarrassed, he sat back. "Sorry, punkin'. I'll let you be miserable, then."

She rolled her eyes, but at least she was interacting with them now, instead of just folding her arms and staring off into space. Cathy smiled at him.

"There's the Pattersons," she said to Julie, pointing to the far door. "Do you think Sara came with them?"

Julie was off like a shot, weaving through the chairs and spectators to look for her friend.

"She's probably going to commiserate about how embarrassing fathers are to take out in public," Cathy said, smiling at him.

"Probably," Chuck agreed, settling back. "Do you want me to take Little Bob? At least he loves his daddy, don't you, big guy?"

But Little Bob clung tightly to his mother, and Chuck sat back, mock pouting. "Nobody loves me."

"I love you, Daddy," Felice said, patting his knee.

Chuck smiled at her. "Thanks, Felice. I love you, too."

But the girl's attention was already gone. "Mom, can I go play with Timmy?" she asked, already half out of her chair.

"Don't leave the room," Cathy called after her. Felice didn't give any indication that she'd heard, prompting a sigh from her mother. "I hope she doesn't get into too much trouble."

"Trouble? That one? Never."

Cathy laughed heartily. "Well, she's not as bad as Ben was at that age. It's a good thing we were younger then; I couldn't keep up with one like him now."

Chuck grimaced at the memories. "Too true. But he turned out all right."

"So far." Cathy looked down at the knot of boys around the track. "Most of the dads are down there. You probably should be, too."

"Should I?" Surprised, he looked again and saw the fathers standing just behind the sons, tinkering with the derby cars to make sure they were just right. "Guess I still haven't quite got the hang of this Scouting thing."

Cathy put her hand on Chuck's arm as he rose. "I'm glad you came tonight. It means a lot to Ben."

He smiled at her. "It means a lot to me, too."

"Well, just remember that when he completely ignores you down there," Cathy warned. "He and Julie are both getting to be too cool for parents."

He hid a twinge of sadness under another smile. "I'm tough. I'll survive."

He made his way down to the area where the fathers congregated. He looked around, a little unsure of himself. Several of them had special toolkits and were making minute adjustments to their sons' cars. Others were showing off the cars with as much pride as if they'd made them all themselves. He overheard one conversation:

"So I added a special axel, and on our tests, it runs twenty percent faster than the old ones!"

I am so far out of my depth here, he thought. He and Ben had followed the directions in the kit to put together the car. The most time they'd spent on it was painting it. He hoped that Ben wouldn't be too disappointed with his effort.

"Chuck!" He turned to see Dave Patterson bearing down on him. "It's good to see you! It's been too long since you were at a Scout activity!"

"Yeah, I know." Chuck winced as his hand was locked in Dave's grip, as usual. "I can see that I need to come more often. I've never been to a Pine-wood Derby before."

"Never?" Dave looked momentarily surprised, and then recovered smoothly. "Wonderful! You'll love it. It's pretty simple—we set the cars at the top of the track, and the first one across the line wins!" He pointed to the long wooden slope on the main table. "Some of these guys get really into it, but it's really just to have fun, you know?"

Chuck grinned wryly. "I may know, but do the boys?"

Dave shrugged. "That's what we're trying to teach them, anyway. I try not to get carried away building my sons' car for them—even if I could do a better job than they could! None of them has ever won much, but we go out for ice cream afterwards, and they mostly seem to be enthusiastic all the same."

Chuck made a mental note. "Good to know. Well, Ben should be in the same boat as your sons; I'm afraid I wasn't much help to him on building the car. I was never any good at woodshop."

They both laughed. Then Dave glanced at his watch. "Ooops, time to start. Tell Ben I said 'good luck,' " he offered, moving to the center of the room and raising his hands for silence.

Ben made his way over to Chuck's side. "Do you think it's ready?" he asked anxiously, lifting the car up to him.

Chuck didn't have the faintest idea how he'd know, but he took the car and looked it over, trying to act professional. He spun a wheel and prodded at the weights they'd added to the front. "Looks like it's in perfect shape to me," he said confidently.

"I'm so excited!" Ben beamed. "Everyone who's done it before says it's awesome. I hope I win!"

"I hope you do, too." Chuck didn't have the heart to dampen his enthu-siasm. "You'd better get in line for the weigh-in, though."

As Ben ran off, he sighed. *If only this would all work out well for Ben*, he thought.

He watched the weigh-in anxiously, relieved to see that the car met the requirements. They hadn't had a very exact scale to work with. He'd tried to arrange the weights so you could take one off or add another if necessary, but he hadn't been able to figure out how to do it. He'd been in a hurry that night, so they just superglued them on. It was a good thing they'd hit the right weight.

At least they didn't have long to wait. The Webelos were the first to race. Chuck watched anxiously as they lined their cars up across the top. Ben's was certainly flashy—he'd gone for red, with yellow lightning bolts up the side. Or maybe flames, it wasn't entirely clear to Chuck. Either way, it stood out in the middle of the track.

At the whistle, they released the cars. They left the starting line together but quickly separated. Chuck's heart sank as he saw the red car dropping back behind two, then three of the others. He hoped that Ben wouldn't be too disappointed.

He watched Ben, instead of the cars, as they headed for the finish line. All the boys were jumping up and down and cheering their own cars on. In fact, Chuck realized that no few of the fathers were doing the same thing. They were the ones in Scout shirts, who'd obviously been doing this their whole lives. Chuck was glad that his son would grow up with this sort of thing; one day, he'd be one of the fathers who knew exactly what was going on, maybe even a Scoutmaster, rather than just feeling lost like Chuck did.

He'd missed the finish, he realized as the cheers died out. He looked at Ben's face. To his credit, the boy still looked excited. Ben collected his car and returned to his father's side.

"I got fourth!" he announced with pride. Then he peered at the car, spinning a wheel as Chuck had just a few minutes before. "And it's still in good shape. They say sometimes cars fall apart on the track. I hope one does today!"

"Congratulations," Chuck told him. "We should go out for ice cream after to celebrate!"

Ben looked up at him. "Really? Do you have time for that?"

Chuck winced inwardly at his son's unintentional reminder of his work-related absences. "Of course! It's not every day you go to your first Pinewood Derby and get fourth!"

Ben's smile widened. "Awesome!" Then he turned back to the track. "Look, Dad! It's Mike's turn!" He ran forward again to cheer his friend on.

***

Even on the way home from the ice cream shop, Ben was regaling them with the highlights of the evening. Felice and Little Bob were already asleep by then. Julie ostentatiously ignored Ben, her attempts to dampen his enthusiasm a failure. Chuck tried to keep interjecting useful comments, but he was starting to get tired, too.

He saw Cathy looking at him as they pulled into the driveway. "Do you want me to read tonight?" she asked softly.

Chuck shook his head. "It's my turn."

"Are you sure? You look tired."

"I'll be okay. I have to stay up anyway to do some work."

"You still have work?" She looked surprised. "Well, thank you."

That comment made him feel so good that he almost didn't regret having to stay up late to finish the proposal. "You're welcome," he said as they carried the kids inside.

As he laid Felice into her bed, he brushed a kiss on her cheek. "I love you," he whispered.

"Loveyou," Felice slurred, cuddling deeper into her covers.

Chuck settled down with Ben & Julie to read the next chapter of *The Lion, the Witch, and the Wardrobe*. It was one of his favorites but he found himself struggling a few times to stay awake. Ben had to poke him once to make him turn the page. When it was over, they hugged him and headed off to bed quickly. "Night, I love you!" floated back.

"I love you," he called after them. That's why I'm doing this now, he reminded himself, dragging himself downstairs to tackle the proposal. He'd been on such a roll when he'd left work, he'd wanted to keep going, but he knew that if he did, he'd miss the derby. He stared at it blankly for a moment. Now he couldn't even remember why he'd been so enthusiastic about finishing it then.

He took a deep breath. Maybe a snack would help him stay awake. He poured himself a glass of milk and pulled a cookie from the cupboard. Then he sat down to stare at the paper again.

As he reread what he'd already written, he wondered why he'd thought it was so easy. The words didn't seem to flow at all. He wondered if he should just put the whole thing off till tomorrow. But he'd need the time tomorrow to go over it with Jess and Raj, and he had to get some work done on the actual project, too.

With a sigh, he picked up his pen and started writing. Once he started, the words began to flow again. It didn't take as long as he'd feared to fill out the rest of the page.

He tossed his pen to the table and rose. Tomorrow would tell whether it was any good. For now, he was finished, and he was going to bed.

20

As he pulled into the parking lot that afternoon, Chuck scanned for Tony's car. There it was, a Cadillac Escalade, parked near the entrance, as usual, gleaming in the sun. He must have waxed it over the weekend; it practically glowed. Chuck ran an appreciative hand over the hood as he walked by; it was a beautiful machine.

Then his worries returned, jostling him from his reverie. This was it. Tony was there, he had gotten the proposal, and he would be waiting with his answer. Chuck steeled himself as he walked through the double doors. The stress, the waiting was brutal. He was glad that he'd have the answer soon.

In the door to his own office, he paused. Everyone was busy at their own tasks. Even Henrich was there, glowering at the screen as he typed. Chuck wondered if Tony had come down on him again. He couldn't blame Henrich for wanting to keep his mobility; he'd love to work on other projects, but Tony was restricting him.

He took a step into the room and chairs swiveled to face him. Jess offered a tentative grin.

"Well, mate? What's the word?" he asked, head tilted in inquiry.

Chuck shrugged. "I just got back from a meeting. I thought you'd know."

"Haven't asked," Jess said sourly. "He came in looking like someone was in for a chewing out, so I kept my head down. So you haven't seen him at all?"

Chuck shook his head. "I left the proposal with Raj. Do you think he got it?"

Jess furrowed his brow, but nodded. "Yeah, he went and talked to Raj a minute before he locked himself in his office."

Chuck nodded. "That's good, then." He headed to his own desk and sat down.

"What?" He turned his chair to see Jess still staring at him. "You aren't going to go ask him?"

"I wasn't planning on it." Chuck pulled his laptop from of its case.

"Well, whyever not?" Jess demanded. "Don't you want to know?"

"Yes, of course," Chuck said. And his impatience started to gain steam; he started to think that maybe Jess had a point. "But I don't want to barge in there when he's busy," he said aloud, trying to convince himself. *Especially when he looks like he's in a chewing-out mood*, he thought. "He'll come tell us when he's ready."

Jess stared at him for a moment and then shook his head in disgust. "I don't believe you, mate. Where's your natural curiosity?"

Chuck shrugged. "Curiosity killed the cat, you know," he said lightly.

"Oh, come off it," Jess said. "You want to know just as much as I do. You're just scared."

"I am not!" Chuck retorted instantly. Then he turned crimson with embarrassment when he realized how juvenile his outburst sounded.

"Are so!" Jess answered. Apparently, he had no qualms about acting like a child.

"Don't be ridiculous," Chuck said, trying to maintain some dignity by using a four-syllable word. "Come on, Jess, let's just work on this project and wait to see what he says."

"Screw the other project! Don't you see, if he accepts this proposal, all that work will be moot anyway? I have no intention of wasting any good, hard work, mate," Jess said firmly. "We need to know now, or we'll never get everything done."

Chuck sighed. He would much rather have this waiting over with, but barging into Tony's office demanding answers still wasn't something he was comfortable with.

"Let's go," Jess said, standing up decisively. "See, mate, I'll even come with you."

Chuck shook his head and rose tentatively. "I'm not sure this is a good idea," he said one more time.

Jess rolled his eyes. "Of course it's a good idea! Come on."

Chuck made his way around the conference table, running a nostalgic hand over the whiteboard. They'd left all their old conversations up there; no one had gotten around to erasing it yet, and after all, you never knew when you'd need to reference one of those old notes. He smiled at the bright colors of his name that still stood out from the first time Jess had left him a message there.

"What are you doing, mate? It's not fording the Amazon or anything. Let's get a move on, here."

Chuck looked down and realized that he was on the edge of a puddle left over from a recent rainstorm. Grateful for the warning, he took an awkward leap across it. His foot came down on the edge with an unpleasant "squish" as he regained his balance.

"Maybe we should ask Raj to come with us," he said as he caught up with Jess. "He's been in on this, too."

Jess glared, but, to Chuck's surprise, didn't argue. He turned toward Raj's door and pounded on it. "Come on. We're going to beard the lion in his den and wrest some answers from him."

Raj said something that Chuck didn't catch. Either Jess didn't either or it was uncomplimentary, because all he said was, "Never mind that, mate, let's get going."

Chuck joined them just as Raj stepped out. Raj smiled at him. "Were you dragged into this 'adventure,' as well?"

Chuck nodded with a small sigh. Raj laughed. "All right, then, here we go. On with the bearding and the wresting."

Jess started laughing just as he knocked. Stepping back, he waved Chuck forward, unsuccessfully constraining his mirthful snorts.

Tony opened the door and looked them over, raising an eyebrow at the chortling Jess. "Yes?"

"We were just wondering if you'd made a decision on that proposal," Chuck said, his voice sounding more uncertain than he would have liked.

"Right," Tony said. "Come on in."

Chuck led them into the office, taking the seat farthest from the door, which Tony closed behind them. Then he sat down at his desk.

"I have good news and bad news," he said, meeting each of their eyes in turn. "I like the proposal. I think it will help the company, and I'm willing to try and implement it before Thanksgiving."

Jess let out a whoop and reached out his hand to Chuck for a high-five. Unable to stop grinning, Chuck returned the gesture. He was excited that Tony liked the idea that much, but he was a little worried about the bad news.

"Unfortunately," Tony cut off Jess's excited commentary, "I'm afraid I'm going to have more trouble convincing the director. He's very fond of this project, you see, and I don't know how he'll take an attempt to change it. I tried to get in to see him this morning, but he's 'too busy;' he says I can't meet with him until next week."

"Next week!" Chuck felt his grin dissolve. Next week was the week before Thanksgiving. There was no way they could pull this off if it took that long to get approval.

"I'm not going to just let that stand," Tony assured them, "but we have to assume that that's the soonest I'll get to have a real conversation with him. And, as I said, I don't know if he'll accept it even then."

Chuck sighed, but nodded. He still hoped that the proposal would pass, but he began to relinquish his hopes of spending Thanksgiving with his family.

"Now, let me get this straight," Jess said. "This bloke knows how much of a time crunch we're in, and he's telling us we have to wait a week?"

Tony rubbed a hand across his eyes. "Everyone's in a time crunch right now. All these projects must have results to report before Christmas. These last few weeks are crazy. I'm supposed to be in meetings every minute myself; I'm just picking and choosing which to attend."

"So what are we supposed to do until then?" Jess demanded. "Work on this project when we don't have official go-ahead? Or stay with the other project that we all devotedly hope will be cancelled before any of that work is actually used?"

"Stick to the old project," Tony said firmly, eliciting a groan from Jess. "I know, it's not as exciting, but we have to be making progress on that, or the director won't listen to a word I say about this new idea."

Jess grimaced but didn't mount an argument. Raj just nodded. Chuck hesitated, and then asked, "What do you think our chances are, Tony?"

Tony leaned back in his chair, staring up at the ceiling for a long moment, as if the answer was hidden there. "I really don't know," he said finally, looking at Chuck over his glasses. "I don't think the director wants to change horses this late in the stream. On the other hand, I didn't want to change, and you convinced me." He grinned crookedly. "I sent Raj in there to shut you up, you know, not to encourage you."

"You told me specifically to find out whether it had merit and to help them if it did," Raj said, sounding as if he'd been misled.

"Well, I didn't think that this idea they were throwing around would actually have merit," Tony said. "After all, I thought it was just an excuse to get out of working on Thanksgiving. I didn't expect you to be coming up with ideas that rock the foundations of our business!"

Chuck grinned. "Just doing our job," he said. "Rocking foundations, tumbling entrenched ideas—that's what we're here for."

Jess gestured with his hand, tracing a building swaying back and forth before tumbling to the ground. "Kaboom!" he interjected with glee.

"Yeah, yeah, you're great," Tony said casually. "Now get out of here."

They stood up, Jess throwing a cheeky salute. "Sure thing, boss," Jess said. "Got to give you time to sell our earthshaking ideas to everyone else."

21

Tony found himself gnawing on his lip nervously as he stepped into the elevator, and he stopped himself at once. When had he last felt nervous? This should be a piece of cake, he assured himself. The proposal was a great one; any fool could see that. There should be no reason not to implement it.

Unfortunately, as he knew all too well, the directors were not always swayed by reason. Good ideas were not the ones that rose to the top on their own merits. They only made it that far if they had someone to fight for them.

In this case, that someone was him.

He smiled to himself as the elevator chimed and the doors parted. He was a fighter, a crusader—and he liked it. It was even better when he actually had a good idea on his plate, something worth fighting for.

Still, that didn't entirely erase the doubt that he couldn't shake as he walked up to the doorway. He studied the mahogany door for a moment, the embossed nameplate beside it. One day, he would be here, he knew that. He wanted an office like this; he deserved an office like this. And this proposal would help him get there.

The director looked up from his desk upon Tony's knock and entry.

"Oh, Tony," he said, glancing at his Rolex. "Is it that hour already?"

Given that Tony had been pushing every day for an earlier appointment, only to be met with some very creative stonewalling, the greeting was less than he had hoped for. The director shouldn't have been able to forget about him, with the amount of time he'd spent chasing him. But then, it was all part of the game.

He took the seat the director to which the nodded and settled himself comfortably. "You know how time flies," he said lightly.

The director only nodded. "What did you have to show me again?" he asked brusquely.

"A proposal from my team," Tony said. "One that will speed up implementation of new ideas and improve software responsivity to the users." He passed the paper over the desktop. Of course, he'd already e-mailed a copy, but he was fairly certain the director wouldn't have bothered to read it. No, this would be his first and only chance to convince him.

The director skimmed quickly over the page, raising his eyebrows at a few sentences. When he'd finished, he looked it over again, more slowly. At last, he laid it carefully down in front of him.

Tony waited silently, his face carefully blank.

"Hhmpf," the director snorted. "Interesting ideas you've got here," he said more loudly.

Tony inclined his head, still waiting.

"Seems like it would be popular, making all those changes little by little, rather than shutting the whole system down for a few days and then leaving people to figure out the new programs overnight."

Tony nodded again. The director still hadn't asked any questions, so he would keep silent as long as he could.

"And, of course, it'd cut out working over public holidays to do installations." The director shot him a keen glance to which Tony was careful not to respond.

"What's working on this idea doing to your progress on your scheduled products?" the director demanded abruptly.

Tony shrugged. "We're still on schedule to complete the upgrade over Thanksgiving weekend, if necessary. We haven't stopped that at all. This is just something we were talking over on the side."

"Hmm." The director looked down at the proposal again. "But it would make that upgrade obsolete if it was approved, wouldn't it?"

Tony nodded slightly. "Replacing it with a better system," he said blandly.

"Yes, of course." The director drummed his fingers against his desk. "But you would want to cancel the other project, then?"

"It would certainly make more sense," Tony said. "It seems useless to do a big upgrade while simultaneously ironing out the last little wrinkles in how to never again have to perform such an upgrade."

The director didn't respond immediately. "It is an interesting idea," he repeated at last, gazing off to the side. Then his attention snapped back to Tony. "I'll have to think about it."

Tony recognized that tactic easily enough. "I'll tell you later" nearly always meant "no," especially if it didn't come with a hard deadline.

"There is a board meeting this Friday, I believe," he said, trying to sound casual. "Will you let me know before then if you're planning to pitch the idea? I have some more information that might help you."

"Yes, yes, of course," the director said off-handedly. "I'll let you know." He rose and walked around his desk to shake Tony's hand. "It's good to talk to you, Tony," he said with a robust smile. "You always have such interesting ideas." He slapped a hand down on the proposal on his desk. "I'll have to think about it, of course."

"I'll be hearing from you later this week, then?" Tony pressed gently, heading for the door.

"What? Oh, right, right, of course. I'll get back to you." The director smiled as he headed out.

Tony's own smile faded as the door closed solidly behind him. He ground his teeth. What a ridiculous situation. Why couldn't the director let this proposal stand on its own merits, rather than always clinging to the old plans? But there was nothing more he could do. He headed back to his own office to tell the team.

***

Chuck tapped his fingers idly on his keyboard. He knew he wasn't accomplishing anything, but he couldn't concentrate. He wasn't sure who had figured out that Tony was pitching the proposal to the director today, but he wished they hadn't. The suspense was a killer.

He looked up eagerly as someone came through the door, but it was only Henrich, back from one of his other activities. Chuck looked back at the project overview on his screen. He was supposed to be rehearsing the training for the user test group who was getting the software in a matter of weeks, but he couldn't focus. He supposed that Jess was right. It was easier not to waste the work if you didn't know if it would even be needed.

Another shadow fell across the door, and he looked up again, but it was Jess clutching yet another cup of coffee. He glanced around the room and smiled when he saw Chuck. "You look about like I feel, mate," he said, sitting down on the conference table next to him. "Want a cup of Joe?"

Chuck smiled but shook his head. "No, thanks. That won't help me concentrate."

"Can't think why not, mate. It's the only thing that helps me." Jess took a long sip from the cup.

Chuck looked back at his computer. "Yeah, well, I'm supposed to be working on this presentation. I really should try to concentrate."

Jess made a rude noise. "Yeah, right. You can try, mate, but it ain't gonna happen."

Resolutely, Chuck turned to face the screen, but he immediately swung around again when he heard the elevator chime in the hall.

Jess started to laugh. "You're as jumpy as a mouse in a convention of cats," he said, shaking his head at Chuck. "Calm down! It's not the end of the world."

Chuck didn't have a chance to respond before Tony walked through the door. His attention was obviously elsewhere as he made his way along the conference room, dodging pulled-out chairs and rain puddles with absentminded grace. But somewhere along the way, their intense stares caused him to pause.

"Sorry, guys," he said softly, shaking his head. "He doesn't want to risk it." Then he turned and continued for his office.

Chuck felt his stomach drop. This couldn't be it! They'd worked too hard on this proposal to have it cut back now, on a director's whim. Tony hadn't even told them why!

Jess stood up suddenly and dragged Chuck with him. "Come on, mate. Let's find out what happened," he said with a resolve in his voice that surprised Chuck.

"Are you sure...?" he faltered, looking at the closed door.

Jess muttered a profanity and headed down the walkway. "Of course I'm sure, mate. We have to know what happened. We need to go in there and ask him what's going on. It's stupid to reject that proposal; you know that as well as I do. I want to know what's going on!"

Chuck followed reluctantly. "Well, maybe now isn't the best time."

"No time like the present." But Jess didn't sound as jovial as he usually did when citing proverbs. "I want to know, mate. And the only way to know is to ask."

Chuck wanted to protest, but he wanted to know what had happened as much as Jess did. He was raging internally at the loss of his idea. He'd worked so hard on that proposal, and the directors just tossed it aside? He straightened his shoulders and readied for a confrontation.

"You're right, mate," he said, mimicking Jess. "I want to know what's going on here."

Jess grinned at him conspiratorially as he knocked on the door. "Way to go, mate. We'll find out something, at any rate. And maybe it'll even be useful. You never know."

Chuck hung back as they entered the office, letting Jess take the lead. He still wasn't entirely sure that this was a good idea.

"What do you need?" Tony asked, sounding almost normal as he smiled at them.

Jess shrugged. "We just wanted to ask what happened with the director."

"I told you," Tony said, looking away. "He blew me off. We're not getting anywhere with him."

"Yes, but why?" Jess asked, his tone betraying fragile patience. "We'd like some details down here, Tony."

Tony rubbed his temples, and then shook his head quickly as if to clear it. "Oh, he didn't give any real reason. Just said that he needed to think about it, all that."

Chuck broke in then, confused. "But if he's going to think about it, what's the problem? Why are you so sure it's not going anywhere?"

Jess and Tony gave him identical patronizing looks. "It was the way he said it," Tony explained. "He obviously had no intention of actually looking into the idea."

"But why not?" Chuck's frustration was overflowing. "It's a great plan! We all know that."

"Oh, of course it is," Tony shrugged. "He even knows that, I imagine. He liked the idea. He just doesn't want to deal with it right now."

"What?" Chuck sputtered, his brow furrowing as he tried to follow that twisted train of logic.

Tony sighed. "Look, Chuck. He had to argue to get funding for our current project, remember? And we've extended the deadline again and again. If he tries to change the project at this late date, people will think it's because we couldn't meet the deadline again and we're trying to get out of it."

"But that's ridiculous! If we couldn't meet the deadline, we'd just extend it, again, like we always do. Not spend our time coming up with a new, better idea!"

Jess spread his hands wide. "What can you do, mate? It's the way of the world."

Tony nodded. "Even if it doesn't make sense, people would still point fingers at him. Directors aren't a circle of friends, you know, Chuck. They're out there trying to outdo each other for the best chance."

Tony actually looked enthusiastic about that state of affairs, which sickened Chuck. He shook his head helplessly.

"Anyway," Tony continued, "if he accepted a change in our project status, he'd have to renegotiate his yearly goals with the vice president. It's already November! That's a little late for new New Year's resolutions. He'd rather just wait until next year."

Chuck looked up at that. "So we might get to implement it next year?"

Tony raised his eyebrows. "Who can say?" He spread his hands helplessly. "Maybe. But of course, by then there will be all kinds of new pressures on the director, new ideas pushing for his attention, new assignments and goals from the vice president. Most likely this one would just fall by the wayside."

Chuck was so angry he was having trouble sitting still. "This is impossible!" he burst out. "We can't even implement a good idea that will help the company because of department politics? It's like a nightmare!"

Jess put a steady hand on his shoulder. "Don't get too caught up in it," he said soothingly. "It's just another proposal. There're thousands of them a year that get lost like this."

Chuck glared at him. Jess shrugged. "Our only other choice is to out-politic them, and Tony already tried that."

Chuck took a deep breath and exhaled slowly. "So…this is it?" he said, looking at Jess for some sort of reassurance.

Jess nodded. "Sure looks that way."

Chuck turned back toward Tony. "Thanks for all your help," he started to say, but stopped at the expression on the man's face. Tony looked like he was struggling with a new idea.

"It might not be," he said at last. "There is something I can still try."

Chuck and Jess exchanged a glance. "Really? And what's that, then?" Jess drawled.

"Out-politic them." Tony grinned suddenly, a feral, teeth-baring leer. "I'm not going to give in that easily to being stonewalled! I can run circles around him."

Chuck glanced at Jess again, a little concerned, but Jess was smiling. "Oh, really? Is that what you think?"

"I know it." Tony was practically grinding his teeth, and Chuck nudged Jess, trying to tell him to stop pushing. Jess threw him a wink.

"Haven't seen it yet, mate," he said casually, picking up his coffee mug.

"You will," Tony said resolutely. "I'll show him that he can't just ignore me like that. I'll go over his head, speak directly to the vice president."

"That sounds like a good idea," Jess said calmly, nodding and taking a sip of his coffee.

"The vice president is sensible," Tony went on. "He'll see the benefits of this proposal. He doesn't have to worry about other people thinking he's wimping out on the old idea because he wasn't directly involved in it."

"Sounds perfect." Jess sounded slightly bored.

"He'll see why it's a good idea," Tony repeated. "Then he can put pressure on the director, and I won't have to try and push my way up; they'll meet us."

Jess nodded and stood up. "We'll leave you to it, then," he said, dragging Chuck to his feet. "Thanks for your time, Tony."

"Anytime." Tony waved a hand languidly at them, his attention still fixed on his own challenge.

22

Tony didn't even try to deny that he was a bundle of nerves as he waited outside the office. He'd been much more on edge lately since taking on this project, more than he ever remembered being before. But it was more than a little risky to go over the director's head and speak directly to the vice president. If this didn't work out, and the director found out about it—well, Tony might spend the rest of his career in limbo, managing some very boring, hopeless projects. And that did not fit in with his plans at all.

He looked down at the proposal in his hands again. It was a good one, he was sure of that. That was the only reason he was willing to stick his neck out like this. He just had to keep reminding himself of it.

His head craned to attention as he heard footsteps inside the office. Voices resonated; he recognized the vice president's deep baritone. Then more footsteps toward the door. Tony hurried to the water fountain nearby, pretending to take a drink.

His peripheral vision caught the vice president exiting the office. Tony abruptly straightened.

The vice president acknowledged him casually. Tony fell in step beside him, heading for the elevators. He could see the vice president peering at him uncertainly out of the corner of his eye.

"It's Tony, isn't it?" the vice president said at last. "It's good to see you again, Tony. This isn't your usual haunt."

Tony smiled politely. "No, I'm afraid not. But I wanted to ask you if you'd heard anything about this yet."

He passed over a copy of the proposal. The vice president looked over it quickly.

"No, I can't say that I have," he said, folding the paper and stuffing it into his computer case. "Looks interesting, though."

"We're finding it very interesting," Tony affirmed. "It looks like it would increase productivity by at least twenty-five percent, probably more, if the system was more responsive to users' needs and changing technologies."

The vice president raised his eyebrows. "That is impressive. I don't know why I haven't heard about it before."

Tony took a deep breath. "Well, it's still in the planning stages," he confessed. "The director doesn't feel that we have enough time to finish the projects we have in place before the end of the year and work on this, too."

"And is he right?" The vice president stopped outside the elevator doors and locked a piercing gaze on Tony.

Tony only shrugged, smiling slightly. "Probably. If we want to do things the way they ought to be done. But it seems to me that we should focus our time and energy on the things that are of the most benefit to the company, even if that means changing some plans."

The elevator chimed, and they stepped in. The vice president pushed the button for the ground floor and the doors slid quietly closed.

"That seems sensible," the vice president said. "But it can be problematic to abandon plans, especially late in the season."

Tony shrugged again. "Perhaps. Sometimes you have to take risks, though."

"But who can tell which risks to take?" The doors chimed again and the vice president stepped out. "I'll have to talk to your director about it. It's the board that decides what risks to take, remember that."

Tony nodded. "Of course." He lagged behind, allowing the vice president to precede him out of the building. As soon as the door closed behind the vice president, Tony leaned against a nearby wall, wiping sweat from his brow.

"Whew," he blurted. "That went...better than I'd expected."

He stopped and glanced quickly to see if anyone had seen him talking to himself. Luckily, he was alone.

He straightened his shoulders, confident that he had done everything he could. There was nothing to do but wait.

And he hated waiting.

Tony headed back to his car, whistling to himself. If he had to wait, he was going to put the best possible spin on it. And after all, it just might work.

***

Once again, Jess was waiting to ambush Tony. "He was going to see the vice president, I know he was," he told Chuck yet again.

Chuck tried to concentrate on his assignment. It wasn't easy with Jess nattering away at him. "I'm sure you're right," he said, frowning at the screen.

"I mean, he had the proposal and everything. What could be taking so long?"

"Who knows?" Chuck muttered, typing a few changes into the presentation.

"Are you even listening to me?" Jess huffed from behind him.

"Sure," Chuck said, his attention focused on the task at hand. "Just not very hard. I'm trying to get this presentation done, all right? I have to present it tomorrow."

Jess reached over Chuck's shoulder and pushed the lid of his laptop shut.

"Hey!" Chuck yelped, barely snatching his hands from the keyboard in time. He spun and shot a glare at Jess.

Jess returned it. "You," he informed Chuck firmly, "are impossible."

"What?" Chuck shook his head incredulously. "I'm impossible?"

"You're preparing a presentation for an upgrade we're not even going to do, and you've been over it who knows how many times already, and you're still concentrating on it. That's ridiculous!"

"At least I'm doing something," Chuck retorted. "We both have work to do, if you'll recall. We're not just here to grab Tony as soon as he walks through the door."

Jess brushed that aside. "I do my work. I just don't obsess over it the way you do. Especially when I know we're not actually going to use any of it. Why don't you take a break once in a while?"

Chuck counted to ten, slowly, trying not to let himself be goaded into saying what he really thought of Jess's work ethic. "I do," he said curtly, turning back to his computer. "Just not right now."

Jess was silent behind him, so he tried to go through the presentation one more time. But somehow knowing that Jess was glowering behind him, even if he didn't say anything, made it even harder to concentrate than being pelted with his complaints. Chuck shook his head grimly and forged onward. At least he could look over the slides one more time and catch any errors or other potential pitfalls.

He felt Jess stiffen behind him, the sudden tension from the other man radiating across the room. Reflexively, he looked up. Tony had just walked in. He looked marginally better than after his discussion with the director; he was still absent-minded, but his head was up and he walked with a firmer step. Chuck found himself feeling a little hopeful.

"So? How'd it go?" Jess demanded, too impatient to wait.

Tony glanced at him and raised an eyebrow. "How did what go?"

Jess rolled his eyes. "I'm not stupid, mate. Any fool could see that you were going to talk to the VP. What did he say?"

Tony shrugged. "I think he liked the idea."

"But?" Chuck prodded, joining the conversation in spite of himself.

"But he wouldn't tell me for sure—just that he'd talk to the director." Tony wiped his forehead, one of the most outwardly nervous gestures Chuck had ever seen from him.

Jess snorted. "What's the director going to think of that, then?"

"I have no idea," Tony replied, his voice displaying only the slightest hint of stress. "I hope it all goes well, or I may have just given this idea the kiss of death."

Jess took a long swallow from his coffee cup. "Don't worry, boss," he said with a wink. "We all know you did everything you could. And personally, I still think that talking to the VP was a brilliant idea."

Tony smiled weakly. "Yeah, well, we'll see, won't we?" His gaze fell on Jess's coffee cup. "You must be rubbing off on me, Australian," Tony said. "I think I'll go get myself a cup."

"Yeah, sure," Jess called after him in his thickest accent. "Blame it on the Australian bloke." Tony's snort of laughter echoed back as he headed down the hallway.

Chuck turned back to his computer, but he couldn't focus on the screen. It was really getting close to the end now. How much longer could they wait under the strain?

23

Chuck sat back in his chair and looked around the dining room table. The kids were still chasing peas around their plates; Cathy had refused to let them leave until every last one was eaten. Julie was pouting more than eating; Ben was hunting down and stabbing each pea viciously.

He looked over at his laptop case, weighing his options. It was only seven o'clock; he could get a few hours of work done on the new idea if he tried.

But he didn't have to. That was just habit. He hadn't realized how often he found work to do after dinner just because he always had work to do at that time. He turned back to the kids. "Anyone want to play a game with me?"

"A game?" They looked dubious.

"What kind of game?" Julie asked suspiciously. "Not a race to see who can eat ten peas the fastest or something."

Chuck tried not to laugh at that idea. "No, nothing like that," he assured her. "A board game or a card game, whatever you guys want. I just thought it would be fun.

Julie and Ben traded looks; Chuck couldn't quite decipher them. "I was gonna go on the computer," Ben said.

"No! I need it for my homework!"

"Then why didn't you do it when you were on the computer before dinner? It's my turn."

"My friends weren't on then. Anyway, I have homework, so you don't get a turn."

"Okay," Chuck broke in. "Ben and I will play a game while Julie does her homework. Then when you're done, Jules, you can come play with us."

Neither child looked overjoyed with this suggestion, but they stopped arguing. Julie shoved the last of her peas into her mouth. "May I be excused?" she said, and then left the table without waiting for an answer.

Ben continued his hunt-and-stab method long enough for Chuck to rinse his and Cathy's plates and put them in the dishwasher. He then cleared the table and sat down across from his son, who still had five peas to go.

"Come on, finish those off so we can play," Chuck urged.

Ben deliberately chased a pea across the plate and back again with a tine of his fork. "What are we going to play?" He didn't sound very interested.

"Whatever you want. What's your favorite?"

He glanced over his shoulder. "All my favorites are on the computer."

"Come on, you must have at least one board game you like."

Ben sighed. "Fine. Let's play 'Sorry.' "

Chuck heard footsteps behind him and turned to see Felice there. "You want to play too, little lady?"

Felice nodded, and Ben groaned. "No, Dad! She never plays right, and she cries when you 'Sorry' her."

Chuck scooped up Felice and propped her on his knee. "It's okay. We'll have fun."

Ben stabbed aggressively at his last pea; it popped out from under his fork and off the plate, rolling under the table.

"Looks like you're done," Chuck said before he could react. "Go rinse your plate; I'll get the game."

As they played, Ben started to loosen up and have fun. Chuck managed to bribe Felice with candy to keep her from crying. Ben won, which put him in a good mood. Cathy walked in just as they finished.

"Hey, babe. Want to join us?"

Cathy hesitated for a moment, and then shrugged. "I probably have time for one game."

One turned into two, and then three as Julie joined them, taking Felice's place when she got bored. Chuck was surprised when they finally noticed that almost three hours had passed. Cathy hurried the kids off to bed while Chuck put the game away, still smiling.

***

Chuck didn't look up when the door to their new office slammed open the next day; it was probably Henrich in a hurry about something.

"Where's Chandlor?"

That caught Chuck's attention in a hurry. He didn't recognize the voice, but he recognized their director, Kent Frye. His mind scrambled for a moment; what was the director doing here?

Jess was ready with a quick response. "He's in his office," he said, gesturing toward the door.

Frye didn't make it more than halfway around the conference table when Tony emerged to greet him. "Kent! Good to see you," he said genially, as if the director were an old friend who'd dropped by for a visit. "What brings you here?"

"This new plan of yours," Frye said curtly. "Klaus wants it ready to present at the planning meeting December 1st."

"Of course." Tony was still all smiles. "Let me show you what we've cooked up."

Frye shook his head. "I've seen what you've done. It's fine, but it's not enough. I need details! Show me how this new program will take care of data migration and functionality in an actual project; the update you were supposed to have done by now will do fine. I want to know who's going to do what when!" He pointed to the project chart that took up the entire wall between Raj and Tony's offices. "Show me this for the new project."

Tony's smile had disappeared. "By when?"

"December 1st!"

"Kent, be reasonable. That's only a week and a half away."

Frye glared at him. "You were planning to work over Thanksgiving anyway. Do it then."

Tony hesitated, and Frye took advantage of the moment to turn and shove his way past the conference chairs back to the door, exiting before anyone managed to speak.

Predictably, it was Jess who first broke the silence. "Is he mad? The whole point was that we don't have to work over Thanksgiving."

Tony sighed. "Sorry, guys. Looks like we don't have a choice."

"No choice?" Jess's voice boiled with indignation. "What do you mean, no choice? We won't do it!"

Tony shook his head. "Don't be ridiculous, Jess. You know perfectly well why he imposed that deadline, and we're not getting out of it."

"Why?" Chuck asked, hoping to derail the argument, but they only glanced at him.

"His bonus!" Jess spat the words as if they left a foul taste in his mouth.

"Huh?"

Tony sighed. "He obviously worked a deal with the vice president that if he presented the new plan at the end-of-year meeting, he'd still get his bonus. So we have to get it done by then." He was moving toward the door as he spoke. "We were already planning to work over Thanksgiving, like he said. That's still on. Chuck, explain the new project to everyone" He stepped out and closed the door firmly behind him.

A string of profanity from Jess broke the silence. "I should have known better than to think this could work," he grumbled at last, throwing himself back into his chair.

Chuck grimaced at Jess's attitude but forged ahead. "You would explain it much better, Raj, or Jess."

"Not me." Jess turned back to his computer. "I have enough to do, putting this plan into motion."

"You explain it very well, Chuck," Raj said. "Go ahead. Bring the team up to date."

Chuck sighed and looked at Susie, Jon, and Henrich. "All right. It's a way to make the upgrade process more flexible and responsive by doing smaller and more frequent updates. And here's how..."

24

"This is ridiculous, I tell you," Jess insisted. "This pattern doesn't even work for the new method. There is no way to make this chart fit what we'll be doing."

Jess had been preaching the same thing all day. At first, Chuck had tuned him out, concentrating on helping the rest of the team understand the new plan. But as he surveyed the project plan and the implementation process chart, he was starting to think that Jess might be right. How could they represent short implementation cycles on a chart meant to detail every bit of work done in a two-year upgrade?

"There's got to be some way to do it," Susie said, gnawing on her lower lip.

"Raj could probably help us figure it out," Chuck suggested tentatively.

Jess rolled his eyes in mock relief. "Sure he could. He'd just snap his fingers and voila! All our problems are solved!"

"He helped us get the ideas together in the first place," Chuck said, shaking his head at Jess' sarcasm.

Jess turned his back on the group assembled around the chart. "Whatever. I'm not doing this. It's ridiculous, it's unnecessary, and I'm not wasting my time on it."

Jon snorted with contempt. "Right. Leave us doing all the work, as usual. Let's hope the director doesn't care that this plan is going to be a piece of junk, if we even get it done in time."

"We'll get it done," Chuck said, with more confidence than he actually felt. How had he ended up in charge of this project? He wasn't a manager! He didn't want to work with people! How was he supposed to do this?

With a sigh, he pulled the paper back. "Well, as I was saying, step one is capturing the requirements. We need to know the number of people it will take. First are the support staff…"

"How many?" Jon interjected, pen poised.

"What?" Chuck stared at him, and then dismissed the question. "We have them. We don't need to count that."

"We need to list them, still," Jon said stubbornly.

"But they don't go on the cost estimate."

Raj leaned out of his cubicle. "Microsoft Project can do that, easily." They both looked at him in surprise. "I'll show you, if you want."

Chuck shook his head. "Later. Let me finish this overview first. So we have the people, with a leader to organize everything and the staff to collect and manage requirements."

"Next," Jess contrived, smoothly rejoining the group, "we need to define the scope and plan the short implementation cycle. That's where choosing the right leader is imperative. We need him to do requirements analysis, be the liaison with the steering and governance team, manage the configuration of the software application, coordinate testing, administer the application of the software, train the users, coordinate the deployment, and be in charge of user support, as well as managing the overall project."

"Surely, other people can do some of that," Susie suggested.

"Perhaps," Chuck interjected before Jess could get defensive. "Of course, everyone would help with that, but the rest of the team needs to be specialists in CAD integrations, software installation, engineering configuration, change management, document management, corporate system interfaces, supplier integrations...Have I left anything out?"

"I doubt it," Jess said. "That sounds like a fairly comprehensive list."

"Well," Chuck sighed as he leaned back, "that's about as far as we've gotten."

Jon shook his head, but at least he didn't say anything. Susie was studying the chart again. "All right," she said slowly. "We still have four main areas of emphasis: helping the users, development, testing, and implementation. That's the same. But when we start putting in their tasks, the work is off-balance."

Chuck sighed. "I know. Let's just put some in and see what we get."

"How? We don't want to just lose the information we've got," Jon said.

Chuck looked around, hoping for inspiration. Susie walked over to her desk and started rummaging through it.

She came back with a handful of brightly colored items. "Sticky Notes," she said, dropping them on the end of the conference table nearest the chart. "Write the task on a note and stick it where you think it belongs. We can move them around and still preserve what we have below."

"Brilliant! Susie, you're a genius!" She blushed and smiled at Chuck's praise. He then grabbed a pad of Sticky Notes and started scribbling. Soon, the board was festooned with notes.

Chuck stared in discouragement at the kaleidoscope of information. "Well, at least now we can see what we have to work with."

"What we have to work with!" Jon glared at him, Susie, and the board indiscriminately. "All we have is a ridiculous distribution of resources that no director is going to take seriously. Look at this!" He tapped the top row of sticky notes. "The user group is insanely busy while we gather information and decide on the new upgrades, and then they have nothing to do! We're trying to make up work for them, and we're not succeeding!"

"Um…" Susie sought to volunteer an idea, but Jon bulldozed his way over her.

"And the developers have nothing to do until the user group tells them what they've decided, and then they spend all their time working on the new upgrade, until it's ready for testing and they go back to doing nothing! It looks like a problem we didn't know we had but now that we're trying to do things faster, it becomes apparent."

"What if-" Susie started to say, but Jon refused to let up.

"The same thing happens with all the other groups. We're going to have to completely redefine roles and rewrite the whole chart to make this thing work!"

"Or," Susie said, loudly enough that Jon stopped and stared at her, "we could move people between the roles."

Chuck, who'd been doing his best to pretend he wasn't part of this argument, turned to her. "What do you mean?"

She became flushed but soldiered on. "Look, like Jon said, we don't need as many people in user support in the development phase. So we make some of the developers do user support at first, and then as soon as we get to development, they change over. That way, we don't need as many people."

Chuck and Jon just stared at her, and her gaze dropped sheepishly to her feet. "It was just a thought," she muttered quietly.

A hand tapped his Chuck's shoulder, startling him. It was Jess. "That's brilliant, mate. That's just what we need."

Chuck twisted in his chair to look up at Jess. "What do you mean?" He glanced apologetically at Susie. "I'm not following."

124

"You move people!" Jess grabbed the mini-notes that no one had wanted to use and placed a handful of them on the user group row. "You start with all your people here, and then they move—" he shifted all but two of the notes to development "—and move—" he shifted them to testing, again leaving a few behind "—and move." He set the last of the notes on implementation and stepped back to look. "It's a circle! That's why this chart won't work. It's not a linear method, it's a circular one."

Chuck's gaze moved from Jess to the chart. "Circular?"

"Yes!" Jess exclaimed with an enthusiasm that surprised Chuck. "It's a much more efficient use of resources, and it'll allow the cycles be so much shorter. It's brilliant! Well done, you," he said to Susie.

"Oh, I didn't come up with all that," she deigned. "You did."

"You came up with the concept, brilliant lady. I merely fleshed it out." Susie beamed at the recognition of her idea.

"The director's not going to like this," Jon said apprehensively.

Jess waved his concerns aside. "Leave that to me. I'll take care of him."

Chuck started to grin. "If you can do this, Jess, we'll be in great shape."

Jess turned back toward his desk. "If? Wait and see. I'll have this done up, and in jig time, too."

25

The next morning, Chuck was eager to find Jess and see how the project was coming. He cornered him at the break room coffee machine. "Well?" he asked eagerly.

Jess shook his head at him, indicating the need for his morning java. "Are you serious?"

Chuck fiddled impatiently while waiting through his friend's daily coffee routine before urging him back to the office. "So, how's it coming? What can we do to help?"

Jess shrugged but didn't speak until they got back to his desk. Then he sighed and sat, cradling his coffee cup in his hands.

"I thought this was a brilliant idea," Jess said flatly, "but this is crazy."

Chuck felt his heart sinking. "It's not going to work?"

Jess shook his head. "I don't know. I can't get the explanation to make sense on my own. I'm even tempted to ask Raj for help." Chuck shook his head at Jess's epiphany. "I'm serious. He could probably make sense of this mess."

"Well, why don't you ask him?" Chuck asked, trying not to sound desperate.

"Maybe," Jess said, his voice betraying a tinge of doubt.

Chuck hadn't heard anyone come up behind him, and he turned when Raj spoke. "I'd be happy to help, if you don't mind."

Jess's face was a mask of surprise. "Really?"

Raj nodded. "I was listening when you and Susie talked yesterday. It sounds like a very clever solution." He offered a small smile. "I love clever solutions. I'd like to be in on this one."

"Well…" Jess hesitated, and a tense Chuck clenched one hand into a hopeful fist. "All right. If you want. This is where I'd got to."

Chuck slipped away quietly as Raj took a seat beside Jess; they started working together. *This has got to work,* he thought to himself.

***

Jess's dejected expression was obvious as soon as Chuck walked in the door. He was sitting at the conference table, slumped down in a chair, chin nearly resting on his chest. At other times, Chuck might have thought Jess was sleeping, but his eyes were open and alert.

Chuck felt a sudden chill. Not more bad news? If the project fell apart this late…They only had a week left before Thanksgiving. This was their last shot.

"What's wrong?" he asked, taking a seat next to Jess. Chuck felt like his heart was lodged in his throat.

"He doesn't like it," Jess muttered. The words were muffled, but the bitterness was unmistakable.

"He what?"

Now Jess sat up and looked squarely at Chuck. "Tony doesn't even want to look at it! He said we all needed to have our parts of the implementation details done for December 1st, and he didn't want to deal with anything else." He slumped back into his chair with resignation. "All that work," he said in a listless voice. "All for nothing."

Chuck stood up and began pacing. "This is ridiculous!" he bellowed, raking his scalp in a rage. "We have the solution here, a perfect solution, and he won't even look at it? It's impossible!"

"Yeah," Jess said with a brief, bitter chuckle. "Welcome to the world of business, mate. Do what you're told, jump through the hoops, and don't ask questions or come up with your own ideas. And that's what makes us such an economic powerhouse."

"There's got to be something we can do," Chuck said stubbornly. "We've fought it this far. We've accomplished things that we thought were impossible—well, I certainly did."

Jess snorted. "I knew full well they were impossible. But you kept pulling them off, somehow. I guess your supply of miracles just ran out."

"There's got to be some way," Chuck repeated. "Something, I don't know…"

Suddenly, Tony's door swung open violently and crashed into the nearest desk, startling Chuck and Jess. Chuck looked at Jess as Tony stalked out quickly, wondering if their conversation had been overheard. The door had been closed, but even so, they weren't making much of an effort to keep their voices down. But they seemed beneath Tony's notice; his attention seemed locked on something else entirely. When he got halfway down the narrow aisle, he acknowledged Chuck, stopping abruptly.

"Oh, good, you're here," he said with palpable relief. "Look, will you tell everyone that we have a team meeting at..." he checked his watch, "two o'clock? I just got some news from the director—I have to go and see him briefly, and then I need to talk to everyone."

Before they could say a word, Tony was gone.

"What was that all about?" Jess asked at last.

Chuck shook his head. "Looks like bad news."

"What?" Jess demanded. "They're going to make us work through Christmas now?"

"We'll just have to wait and see, I guess," Chuck said, unsure of what fate had in store.

"Lovely. More waiting." Jess stood and headed for the front of the room. "Story of my life." He uncapped the nearest whiteboard marker and tested it. "Nothing, as usual." Finding a working marker, he started writing, taking up the entire board with the following message: "TEAM MEETING 2:00."

When he started adding his usual starbursts and lines, Chuck shook off his apathy and pulled out his cell phone to send a quick text message to Henrich.

In the meantime, he opened his laptop and tried to work on his area of the implementation details, but it was impossible to focus. He finally sighed and sat back. Now that Tony had torpedoed their plan, this report was even more important. But he was far behind, and he couldn't find it in himself to care. What did it all matter, anyway? It was just a hoop to jump through, like Jess had said. Why bother doing his best? He thought bitterly of the plan they had worked so hard on. It just wasn't fair that it should be tossed out so quickly, without even being given a consideration.

His musings were interrupted by Raj's entry. He stopped in the doorway, evidently noting the dispirited energy in the room. "What happened?" he asked.

Jess didn't seem inclined to respond, so Chuck did it for him.

"Tony refused to even consider the new repeatable-steps plan," he said flatly, his voice devoid of emotion.

"What?" Raj sounded outraged.

Chuck sighed. "He won't even look at it. We're stuck with the original implementation details due December 1st."

Raj shook his head angrily. "This drives me crazy! I don't mind working overtime to do something worth doing, but we don't need to get this stuff ready for that meeting! We have everything the director needs!"

Chuck only shrugged and pointed to the whiteboard indicating the two o'clock meeting. "There's more."

Raj considered the message for a moment. "What about?" he asked wearily.

"We don't know," Jess finally spoke up. "He came roaring through here like someone lit his tail on fire and just told us to get everyone together before he ran off."

"He said it was news from the director," Chuck added, "but that's it."

Raj rubbed his eyes. "All right, then," he said finally. "I'll see if I can get some work done on those...implementation details...before then." He sounded repulsed at the thought but headed for his office.

Chuck and Jess quietly turned back to their own work.

***

Amazingly, everyone was back in the office at two, even Henrich, who hadn't been seen for about three days. Chuck didn't question it; he just took his place at the conference table and rested his head in his hands, awash with fatigue. He wished he could just go home for the day. Unfortunately, he didn't think that Tony would be bearing that kind of news.

It was ten after two before Tony strode in and took his place at the head of the table. "Sorry I'm late, everyone," he said. Chuck noted the creases in his brow; they were deeper than usual. Definitely not good news, then.

"This will be brief," Tony continued. "I just have a quick announcement that I wanted to make to everyone at once." He drew a shallow breath. "There's been an emergency in our office in Germany. The vice president has requested that the director and I travel there and deal with it. Immediately." He scanned the assembled faces. "We'll be leaving tomorrow—in the afternoon, I think. I'll probably bring my luggage to work and leave directly. So I just wanted to let you know that I won't be here until next Wednesday."

He cast a second look over his team, meeting each set of eyes. "And that will leave us only a few days before our implementation details are due. I don't think I need to remind you how important it is that they be finished by then."

No one said a word.

"All right, then," Tony said firmly. "I'll be reachable by e-mail if you have a problem, but I expect you to have those details of the implementation nearly done by the time I get back."

Heavy sighs were shared across the room.

"But," Tony added in a vacuous attempt to add some goodwill to the pall, "I think we can cancel the meeting we've planned for Monday. We don't need to worry about our weekly status reports quite so soon. We'll do it after this project is over." He looked around the table one more time, and then slapped his hands down. "All right, that's it. I just thought you ought to know." Without another word, he turned and headed into his office, closing the door behind him.

Chuck massaged the back of his neck, head down. Around him, everyone was turning back to their laptops or, in Henrich's case, packing them up to leave. He didn't want to get back to those implementation details. They didn't seem worth the aggravation anymore.

Chuck then looked up to see Jess grinning at him; he was incredulous. Now what?

"This is it, mate!" Jess whispered. "This is our chance!"

"What?"

Jess rolled his eyes impatiently. "They're going to Europe! Tony and the director, together! They'll have nothing to do in the hotel in the evening, and they'll have plenty of chances to talk—it's the best chance we're going to get to make sure they consider the progressive steps plan!"

Chuck stared blankly at Jess. Then a voice spoke from over his shoulder. "But how are you going to get them to do that? You said Tony refused."

Chuck turned to smile at Raj for bringing up the point he'd been searching for.

"There's got to be a way," Jess said stubbornly. "Look, I'm going to run off some copies of the progressive steps plan."

"Copier's down," Raj warned. "They say they'll have it fixed sometime tomorrow."

Jess cursed and looked around. "Then I'll take it to Kinko's," he said at last. "I'll be right back." He turned and grabbed his laptop.

"But—" Chuck began, still wondering how they were going to get the director to read it.

"Not now!" Jess said, walking past him. "We'll figure out the details later, okay?"

Chuck looked back at Raj, who only shrugged; he returned the gesture. Maybe Jess would think of something. Until then, he had to get back to work. With a groan that he managed to internalize, he turned back to his computer.

26

Chuck whistled as he looked over the plans Jess had handed him. "You sure went all out on these," he said, admiring the heavy laminate covers and solid twist binding.

Jess grinned. "Yeah, I sure hope Tony doesn't mind paying for it. There's still some money left in the budget—I think."

"How much were they?" Raj asked, turning the pages.

"Don't ask!" Jess winked. "Let's just hope they do the trick."

"But how are we going to get them to read it?" Chuck asked. "They're beautiful, Jess, but not quite that beautiful. They're not presenting an irresistible temptation, saying, 'Read me! Read me!' "

"Maybe not here," Jess said with a conspiratorial look. "But on a transatlantic plane ride, I think they'll look pretty engrossing. Or in an ugly hotel room."

"The problem is still getting them onto that plane and into that hotel," Raj said calmly. "Unless, of course, you were planning to mail it to them there."

Jess' grin broadened. "Nope. Got a better idea." Looking around with exaggerated care, he moved quietly to the door. Tony's luggage was sitting there, along with the director's; they were riding to the airport together. "Keep watch," he hissed, waving a hand toward the door as he crouched over the suitcases.

Chuck wanted to smile at the theatrics, but he was more concerned about Jess breaking into the managers' luggage. He moved a little closer to the door and glanced out. There was no one in sight.

Jess stealthily slipped the plans into the carry-on luggage, right on top where they'd be easy to find. Then he straightened up with a satisfied look on his face, dusting off his hands. "Perfect," he announced, grinning at Raj and Chuck. "Now they'll be sure to read them."

Chuck shook his head helplessly. "How many times does this make now, that we've ignored proper procedures, gone over people's heads, and all-around not listened to common sense?"

Raj paused. "Well, let's see. If we count every time you two talked about this when Tony had told you not to, that would mean at least..."

"It was a rhetorical question!" Chuck groaned, laughing. "Well, as long as it works, right?"

"Right." Jess gave him a high five. "And it is working!"

Footsteps were heard in the hall, and the three men scattered, trying to look intent on their own tasks. When Tony grabbed the luggage and waved a general good-bye, Chuck found himself struggling to keep a straight face. He didn't dare look at Jess.

"Have a good trip, Tony," Jess said cheerily.

Chuck ducked his head toward the keyboard.

Tony returned an absent "You, too," and disappeared.

Jess leaned back in his chair and stretched, grinning with triumph. "Operation Takeoff, a success," he announced. He blew on his knuckles and polished them on his shoulder. "Thank you, thank you very much."

"Let's wait and hear the results before we celebrate," Chuck cautioned. But he didn't know just how long they would have to wait.

***

Chuck typed a few more details into his section of the implementation plan and checked his word count again—still pitifully low. He knew now that there was no way he'd make the December 1st deadline. Jess's plan had better work; otherwise, they'd all be sunk. He didn't even want to think about the end-of-year performance review. What, with all the delays and then changing their project in midstream, his total output was abysmally low. He liked to think that an amazing new idea would make up for the lack of numbers, but unfortunately, he knew the system too well. He was sure that data would trump any actual accomplishment.

Behind him, he half-listened as Jess answered his phone. "Oh, hey, Tony."

Abruptly, Chuck sat bolt upright and swerved in his chair to stare at his friend.

Jess was turning idly from side to side as he talked. "Yeah, I'm fine. How are you?" He turned far enough for his eyes to meet Chuck's and gave him a thumb's up sign. "Yeah, everything's going well here. Right on track for the first, I'm sure." Chuck glared at him, eliciting a half-shrug from Jess. "Well, I like to think so, anyway. I like to think positively."

There was a long silence on Jess's end. "Really? A stowaway! You don't say?" Again he smiled at Chuck. "Well, did you take a look at it?" A pause. "Now, Tony, if I thought it was funny, I'd be laughing, wouldn't I? You know I hate to waste a good joke." Another pause. "Yes, well, if that's the way you want to look at it. I rather thought that I was just following in my manager's illustrious footsteps." He listened a moment, then sighed. "Yes, Tony, that one was a joke. What, have those Germans leeched all your sense of humor already? Oh, the director read it, too?"

Glancing back at Chuck, Jess pushed a button on the phone and set it on the table between them. "What did he think?"

Tony's sigh sounded tinny through the tiny speaker. "He was actually impressed at your audacity, I think."

Jess's eyes lit up and he mouthed "Yes!" at Chuck. Aloud he said, "I live to serve, of course."

Tony's snort carried clearly. "Serve yourself, you mean."

Chuck looked up to see that the rest of the team had gathered around the table. Even Raj had come out of his cubicle and was listening intently. It almost seemed as if they were afraid to breathe, waiting to hear the verdict. "Yes, well, I do what I can," Jess said lightly. "So he liked it?"

In the pause that followed, Jess's smile started to slip. Chuck felt his stomach drop.

"Well, to be frank, no," Tony said at last. "He thought it was interesting, but he still needs the detailed implementation plan a week from today."

Jess blanched. Chuck knew that he'd spent so much time on the other project that he'd barely touched the implementation plan details. "But..." Jess said, his retort crumbling into oblivion. There was nothing left to say.

"I'm sorry," Tony consoled with uncharacteristic delicacy. "I know you worked hard on that."

Chuck couldn't stop himself. "It has everything we really need. These other implementation details are just ridiculous."

"Chuck?" Tony paused. "Am I on speakerphone?"

Jess shrugged, apparently forgetting that Tony couldn't see him. "Well, I thought everyone would want to hear." His tone became bitter. "That was when I thought we were getting good news, of course."

"It's a disappointment," Raj said softly.

"Disappointment? It's an outrage," Jon said, echoing the sentiment in the room. Everyone looked at him. "All right, I know that I didn't work on it, not much at least, but I looked it over. It's more useful than most of the useless reporting details I'm churning out. Why am I working absurd hours to get this done when it isn't even necessary?"

Susie sighed. "I had hoped…" she said helplessly, before letting the words trail off. "Oh, well."

Tony sounded haggard. "Look, I know how much you're all putting into this. I appreciate that. But we have to follow the system."

"But that's the whole point!" Chuck said. "We don't have to follow the system! That's the whole reason we did this project, and the only way it got approved."

"I'm sorry," Tony said again. "It's out of our hands now."

There was a moment of silence. Then Jess sighed audibly. "Oh, well," he said. "Guess it's back to work for us." He picked up the phone. "Bye, Tony."

"Je-" Tony's voice was cut off as Jess flipped the phone closed. He looked around the room, meeting each person's eyes in turn, but Chuck couldn't bear it. All for nothing. It didn't seem possible. One by one, the team members drifted back to their workstations. No one said anything. There was nothing to say.

27

As Tony hung up the phone, he was gripped by inexplicable guilt. What was wrong with him? It wasn't his fault that the director rejected the proposal. He'd told them not to try it, not to get their hopes up.

But the dejection he'd sensed over the phone gnawed at him relentlessly. He knew that they were exhausted. It was clear in their voices, even from halfway across the world.

He flipped through the booklet again, idly turning pages. They'd done a nice job with it. But there was no way the director could approve something so different from regular company policy. He didn't have time to understand this new concept; he had to have something he could show the other directors and vice presidents without long explanations.

Tony paused on the page that illustrated their new, cyclical concept in a diagram. The picture reminded him of something. It had been nagging him ever since he'd first flipped through the document. What was so familiar?

Suddenly, it came to him. This was a PDCA diagram—one of the fundamental tenets of a LEAN methodology. The new CEO had explained it to them at the beginning of the year as a new objective. Tony had never bothered to explain it to his team; he thought they would never need it. But here they'd created one on their own. The first step, gathering information from the users to make the requirements, that was clearly the Plan step. Then they developed the upgrade; that was Do. Then they performed testing, the Check step, and finished with implementing the new method and gathering user responses, Act. He could make this into something the director would understand! If he was changing the upgrade process to support the CEO's new PDCA initiative, his bonus would be assured!

Assuming, of course, that Tony could persuade the director of that. He pulled out a pen and got to work.

28

Chuck paused outside the office, steeling himself to enter the room. Lately, he felt as if he'd been living there. It had been good to get away for lunch—despite the looks from his teammates to see him actually dare to leave with the project still unfinished. But the price of that relaxing meal was the sobering realization that he had to return. He took a deep breath and pushed the door open.

The clattering of keys was his only welcome—well, that and the pervasive odor of wet carpeting that he'd almost learned to ignore. He headed for his own desk; no one offered a word of acknowledgement. What fun they were all having, trying to complete an impossible task.

Something hit his arm. He looked down to see a pen cap fall to the ground, then up to meet Jess' eyes. "We've got news," his friend said, sounding grumpy, and gestured to the front whiteboard. In a sober black, each letter filled in to take as much space as possible, it read: Team Meeting as soon as Tony arrives—circa 2:00. Status reports due.

Chuck collapsed into the nearest chair. "What? I thought he cancelled that whole business with status reports."

"Looks like he changed his mind." Jess crumpled an empty disposable coffee cup into a makeshift ball and threw it across the room. It bounced off the wall above the wastebasket and rolled across the floor, disappearing under the table.

Chuck closed his eyes and massaged his temples. "Why now? He has to know that we can't have gotten anything done worth presenting!"

"You'll be fine," Jess said bitterly. "It's me that's been spending all my time working on your useless idea, so my work is the farthest behind."

Chuck bristled at Jess's callousness. "And so all the time I've spent helping you counts for nothing? Or Raj? You think you're the only one behind?"

"We're all going to be even more behind if you two don't shut up and get back to work," Jon said from across the room. They ignored him. "It was your idea in the first place that got us this stupid assignment."

Chuck took a deep breath, trying to keep things in perspective. The time for bickering was over; they needed to work.

"I'm sorry things didn't work out the way we'd planned," he said, fighting to maintain a calm demeanor. "None of us are going to look too great in this meeting, are we?"

"I've half a mind not to go," Susie put in. Chuck turned to look at her. "It's ridiculous, telling us there won't be a meeting and then changing his mind an hour before."

"If he really wanted us to get done, he'd let us keep working," Jess put in. "Maybe we should just boycott the thing. He can't have a meeting if no one shows up, now can he? What do you say, Henrich?"

The programmer glanced at them. "Well, I don't think my information is that important to this new project..."

"Besides which, you miss half the team meetings anyway, so who's to know the difference?" Jess broke in. "Great. Are you game, Chuck?"

Chuck shook his head. "Come on, Jess. We can't skip it."

"Why not? Aren't you the king of only following the rules when they help you out?"

"This is different!"

"Oh?"

Before the argument could re-escalate, Raj opened the door to his cubicle. "Aren't you even curious to see what he'll say, Jess?"

Jess turned to reply but stopped in his tracks.

Chuck gratefully jumped on Raj's redirection. "Yeah, we should go and find out exactly what kind of shape we're in. You never know, something good might come of it."

Jess snorted.

"All right, or we'll just have a chance to see exactly how bad it can get. You don't want to miss one of Tony's scenes, do you?"

Jess rolled his eyes. "As if I cared," he muttered. "All right," he said more loudly, "I'll go. But if he starts trying to blame us for not being done, I might walk out. I give you fair warning."

As everyone turned back to their own computers, Chuck rubbed his head again. Forget trying to be home for Thanksgiving weekend; now he just wanted to survive it.

***

Tony silently surveyed his team. Chuck wondered what he saw. Was their exhaustion and disillusionment evident at a glance? He found himself hoping so. Maybe Tony would at least have some pity on them.

Then he shook his head at his own thought. Pity? Tony didn't know the meaning of the word.

"How did everything go while I was gone?" Tony asked, his tone full of forced good humor. "Are we all still on track for the deadline?"

A dull silence was the only response. Chuck glanced around again, his frustration mirrored on every face. If Tony couldn't come up with something to boost morale, the powder keg was threatening to blow.

Tony started to frame another question, and then paused. He looked down for a second. "I was going to save this for after your reports," he said, "but maybe it'd be better to tell you now."

Chuck couldn't place the tone in Tony's voice. The words sounded muffled, and Tony didn't look up from the pattern he was tracing with his finger on the tabletop.

"As you know, the director and I had a very interesting document to look over while we were in Germany," he said. Chuck bit his lip to maintain his temper. If Tony was going to start telling them off for that, he wasn't sure he could control himself—let alone what Jess would do.

"Unfortunately, he had a few nitpicks that kept him from accepting it." Tony paused a moment. "But I had some free time in the hotel room, so I took a look."

Predictably, Jess was unable to stand the suspense. "Just spit it out, Tony," he drawled. "We've got work to do."

Finally, Tony looked up, and they could see the smile he'd been struggling to hide. "No, you don't," he said.

Chuck stared at him in disbelief.

Tony started to laugh. "You should see the looks on your faces!" He sobered up enough to say, "I made a few changes to that document, and the director accepted it," Tony announced. "He doesn't need the other reports until the new year. You're off the hook. You did it!"

Chuck felt like his brain was trying to swim through Jell-O. He couldn't seem to process the news. Had Tony really said that the director accepted their plan?

"Tony, if this is a joke..." Jess began, his voice wavering slightly as he struggled to complete his thoughts.

"No joke." Tony met Jess' eyes, and Chuck began to actually believe what he'd said. "Happy Thanksgiving, guys."

Jess whooped and tossed his paperwork skyward. Chuck felt a gleeful grin start to crease his face. They'd done it!

After shaking hands and trading a few good-natured pats on the back with Raj, Jess pulled away to congratulate Chuck. "We did it!" he shouted, unable to contain his joy.

Chuck was drunk with elation. "We did it!"

Tony spoke up, tempering the mood slightly. "Calm down, guys. We still have to finish the meeting."

"What for?" Jess laughed, tearing up some of his discarded paperwork. "We're done! We don't have to do this stuff for a month!"

"I still want to know where we're at," Tony said with icy patience. "If you'd all sit down and give me an update?"

Reluctantly, Chuck went back to his seat, feeling his euphoria slip away. He really had hardly anything done. Why did they have to bother with this?

As Tony asked his questions, it became apparent that no one had finished much. Tony frowned at the notes he'd collected.

"There's no way we would have finished this," he said, half to himself.

"Guess what, Tony? We don't have to!" Jess was irrepressible, grinning at them all. "Look, what does it matter? We got enough for the director to go on for Monday. And we'll get the rest done next month. We're not that far behind!"

Tony frowned again. "We really should have more done, even with another month to go..." he began to say, then smiled in spite of himself. "You look like a bunch of first-graders waiting for recess," he said. He shoved the notes into his briefcase. "All right, fine. Go home. Have a good Thanksgiving. And be ready to work your tails off Monday morning! Team meeting, 8 a.m.!"

He had to shout the last; everyone was already making for the door. Chuck could hardly keep his mind in gear enough to answer the excited chatter: "Yes, my wife will be so excited." "I plan to sleep!" "Turkey, here I come!"

As he made his way out the door, Tony stopped him momentarily.

"Congratulations," his boss said softly, with a smile.

"Right back at you," he grinned, and hurried home.

Epilogue

Chuck leaned back in his chair. "Woah! I can't remember the last time I ate so much!"

Julie and Cathy had finished long before, but Felice and Ben were still toying with the last of the pie. He shook his head at them. "You ought to be ready to explode!"

Felice stuck her finger in the whipped cream and licked it off. "Nope," she smacked. "Not yet."

Chuck laughed and looked over at his wife, who was surveying the table with satisfaction. She smiled at him. "I should get up and do the dishes, but I don't want to," she said lazily.

"Then don't." He caught her hand. "They'll keep."

She scooted her chair over to lean against him. "I'm glad you're home."

Chuck surveyed the table of half-empty dishes and the scene before him: Felice and Ben getting stickier with pie; Little Bob asleep in his high chair; and, miracle of miracles, Julie actually relaxing at the table with her family.

"Me, too," he said thankfully. "Me, too."

www.ingramcontent.com/pod-product-compliance
Lightning Source LLC
Chambersburg PA
CBHW071208050326
40689CB00011B/2276